W9-BMQ-398

SHAMANIC WISDOM
Nature Spirituality, Sacred Power
And
Earth Ecstasy

DOLFYN

The ideas in this book are not to be understood as directions, recommendations, prescriptions or advice of any kind. The information in this book is based on traditional and contemporary shamanic and neo-shamanic lore. This book only intends to report that lore. Readers with medical, psychological or physiological problems should consult their physician, psychiatrist or qualified health professional. The author and publisher do not intend that the reader rely on shamanic lore as a substiture for medical, therapeutic, psychiatric or psychological care or advice.

Earthspirit, Inc.
d/b/a Sacred Earth in California
6114 La Salle Ave., Suite 362
Oakland, CA 94611

Copyright © 1990 Earthspirit, Inc.
All rights reserved.
Printed in the United States of America

ISBN: O-929268-16-4

Cover Painting by Larry Wells

SHAMANIC WISDOM
Nature Spirituality, Sacred Power
And
Earth Ecstasy

DOLFYN

Earthspirit, Inc.
d/b/a Sacred Earth in California
6114 La Salle Ave., Suite 362
Oakland, CA 94611

ALSO BY DOLFYN:

CRYSTAL WISDOM: SPIRITUAL PROPERTIES
OF CRYSTALS AND GEMSTONES

SHAMANISM: A BEGINNER'S GUIDE

SHAMANISM AND NATURE SPIRITUALITY:
THE SACRED CIRCLE

BOUGH DOWN: PRAYING WITH TREE SPIRITS

PRAYING WITH FIRE: COMMUNICATING
WITH FIRE SPIRITS

CRYSTAL CONNECTION: FINDING YOUR
SOULMATE

CRYSTAL WISDOM: A BEGINNER'S GUIDE

AUDIO CASSETTES BY DOLFYN:

SHAMANISM: A GUIDE TO DEVELOPING
SACRED POWER

CRYSTAL WISDOM: A BEGINNER'S GUIDE

WORKSHOPS WITH DOLFYN

Dolfyn teaches workshops and classes on Nature Spirituality and Shamanism in the San Francisco Bay area and
nationally. For information, write: Earthspirit, Inc., 6114
La Salle Ave., Suite 362, Oakland, CA 94611

Earthspirit, Inc., distributes **DOLFYN'S BOOKS, BOOK-
LETS, CHARTS AND WALLET CARDS TO WHOLE-
SALERS.** For a wholesale catalogue, send your tax #,
address and $1.00 to: Earthspirit, Inc., 6114 La Salle Ave.,
Suite 362, Oakland, California, 94611

The public can order this book by sending price of book
plus $2 shipping, handling to above address. Try your local
bookstore first. Bulk rates also available.

TABLE OF CONTENTS

CHAPTER I
WE ARE ALL RELATED

SHAMANIC WORLDVIEW

Primal peoples from all over the world, such as Native American Indians and tribal peoples of Africa and South America, hold a shamanic worldview. These people we call indigenous or aboriginal not only live close to the natural world, they live in harmony with it, in balance with all other beings, whom they regard as their relatives. Primal peoples have developed paths of psychic powers and spiritual wisdom that are over thirty thousand years old. These belief systems are variously called Earth Religion, Nature Spirituality or Shamanism.

One fundamental realization must be ours to walk the shamanic path: everything that is natural on the earth is alive and conscious. Bear and Crystal, Cat and Oak, Salmon and Butterfly, Wind and Water all have a wisdom and a consciousness that we can communicate with. In a shamanic worldview, all of Earth Mother's children are

1

related. We are brother and sister to the Wolves and to the Wind, to the Fire and the Birds. We are all one great family.

When we attempt to base our lives on this kind of understanding, when we acknowledge the plants and animals and minerals as our relatives, we re-establish our natural connection to all living beings. Not only do we break out of the isolation we feel when we see the rest of nature merely as objects for our use, we begin to re-enjoy our world, and to experience the earth as a sacred place. And unless we break out of our isolation, we can never hope to communicate with and learn from the Nature Spirits, a primary source of shamanic wisdom and power.

Furthermore, because we understand that Earth Mother is alive and conscious, we revere and honor Her as the giver and sustainer of life. The shamanic path leads us into a loving relationship with Earth Mother. We can pray to Her for guidance, comfort and well-being, for She is our Mother.

When we realize and act on the truths of a shamanic worldview, our life upon Earth Mother becomes enlivened, and filled with a sparkling magic. We can befriend every being on earth. We can learn from their wisdom and be strengthened by their power. And as the youngest species of all the living Earth, we need to do that. We need to experience the ancient wisdom of Earth Mother, bring ourselves into alignment with Her, befriend the spirits that live in all natural places and restore ourselves and our souls to wholeness.

Although each tribe or primal group has different specific elements that are unique to their path, the principles of shamanism are the same. In this book I attempt to distill

We Are All Related

the essence of the shamanic worldview and to teach you how to walk a shamanic path. This book will show you some ways to adopt the shamanic worldview as your own, to communicate with the Nature Spirits in the languages of emotion, humor, love and creativity—the languages they understand. It will show you ways to open yourself to the deep wisdom of nature, to respond consciously and subconsciously to Earth Mother's archetypal symbols and manifestations, to enter into a relationship of love and thanksgiving.

On a shamanic path we are no longer alone. Although we may have a human family, human friends and lovers, we often feel incomplete. We humans tend to look to each other for understanding and help that is so often beyond human capacity to give. But the Nature Spirits, whose wisdom and powers have evolved for so much longer than our own, never let us down. They offer to share with us the power that brings clear water from deep in the rock ribs of Earth Mother, the power that creates the fragile strength of the spider's web, the power that swings the stars through their courses and swells the ocean tides. When we connect ourselves with our extended family of the Nature Spirits, we learn how to be enlivened by their energy and to become wise with their wisdom. That transforms us. It transforms our relations with others. It transforms our world.

Earth Mother is calling Her human children back to the ancient ways of shamanism so that we might heal ourselves and our planet. She beckons us to Her so that we might once again walk in balance and in reverence upon our sacred Earth Mother.

NATURE SPIRITUALITY

In the sense anthropologists use the term, shamanism describes a body of practices and beliefs used by some members of tribal societies for specific spiritual purposes. I use the term more broadly. When I talk about shamanism or a shamanic way of being in the world, I am referring to a spirituality and lifestyle rooted in nature.

The shamanic worldview might better be referred to as Nature Spirituality, the spirituality that sees everything as a reflection of the Great Spirit. At the heart of this spiritual path is the knowledge that all beings (seen and invisible, past and present) are connected in kinship and that the smallest being speaks to us of the greatest mysteries.

On a shamanic path we worship the Creator by honoring the creation. We seek oneness with Earth Mother. We open our hearts to the healing wholeness of nature. We go outdoors often, to experience the seasons, the elements, in an essential way. When we are in nature, we treat Her with respect. Every nature being we meet is a potential friend and a teacher because we know that even the tiniest ant carries the mystery of creation within her soul. We respect, protect and deeply identify with all the creatures with whom we share this beautiful earth.

In this way of understanding shamanism, then, we learn not only through words and techniques but through direct experience. We don't just learn the names of the moon phases, for example, we also experience the power of Moon's changing forces when we live our lives in ways appropriate to those cycles. We do not just discuss the way

We Are All Related

a small stream gradually makes a new channel in the earth and rock, but we experience the changes our own steady perseverance brings into our lives' direction as we learn to communicate with the Water Spirits.

When we spend time in creation, we spend time with the Creator. Expressing our dependence on and appreciation for the creation, we thank the Creator. When we help prevent the destruction of old growth timber or start recycling bottles, we show our reverence for the Creator. When we defend Earth Mother we join the Creator in nurturing and protecting life itself. The entire cosmic mystery abides in each natural being; the entire power of the Great Mystery is present in the smallest action in or on behalf of the web of life.

This spiritual path is about connection with all the living worlds, about relatedness with all beings, about communication with all our relatives—in nature and in the spirit worlds. That's why we have ceremonies and rituals of various kinds—to remind ourselves of the many connections that we enjoy and to make sure we stay open to communicating with the sources of our power and of our very being. And that's also why I'm always urging my students not to let themselves be distracted by getting too caught up in ritual details. Whether one behaves formally or spontaneously in a medicine wheel is far less important than deeply experiencing the reason for having the sacred circle in the first place. And debating the use of cedar as opposed to sage for smudging is useless if we lose track of why cleansing ourselves (our spirits) is necessary. Frankly, the energy spent worrying about ceremonial details like this would be better spent getting ourselves connected with nature or standing up to those who would destroy Her. Therefore, as you apply the shamanic rituals and ceremonies presented here to your own life, feel free to change them in ways that have meaning and beauty to you.

SEEKING GUIDANCE FROM EARTH MOTHER

Shamanic insight and abilities arise and are grounded in the natural world. To develop these capacities, then, you must open yourself to Earth Mother's teachings through constant communication with Her.

The first step in communicating with Earth Mother is a sincere love of Her. Go into nature often, and while there spend some time in quiet contemplation of Her beauty. Speak aloud of your love, your respect and your reverence to all the beings you encounter: Tree, Grass, Flower, Sky, Bird and so forth. You communicate with Earth Mother through your interaction with the varied aspects of Her.

When you speak to Earth Mother, speak simply, from your heart, as you would with a close friend. You can hear Her reply by listening, with your heart, to the voices of the animals, the wind in the trees, the waves and the waterfalls. Sometimes you can hear words, but usually nature will impart Her wisdom in a more intuitive and poetic way. What Earth Mother has to say to you will shape itself as a feeling in your heart, a visualization, a sudden flash of insight or a prompting to pay attention to a particular being in the natural world. You can speak to nature, too—with

We Are All Related

your voice, your thoughts or simply with your presence as you sit quietly with Her. Such frequent, intimate and direct communication with nature is easier than many people suppose.

Speaking With Nature

Begin by going to any place that's removed from the world of man-made things. If you can get into the wilderness, fine, but a park or even a corner of a backyard will do just as well (especially since you can probably get there more often.) Be fully present there. Pay attention to what you hear. Touch the leaves, bark, soil, stones, and grass. Let your hands feel the movement of wind or water. Say out loud any words that come to you, even if you feel a bit foolish doing that, at first. And don't worry about making a flowery speech. Simple expressions of thanks and wonder are every bit as effective as high-flown rhetoric. For instance, you might say something like this: "Oak tree, I appreciate your cooling shade. Thank you for feeding and sheltering the birds."

Then be silent. Wait for a response to come to you in the form of the first thought, feeling or visual image that you have. Finally, thank the nature being you've been communicating with for listening to you, whether or not you perceived a response.

It is from this kind of continual contact with nature that true wisdom, healing and guidance is given humans. All the nature beings of our sacred Earth Mother are evolutionarily older than humans, and have great wisdom to share with us. We can always seek guidance from them.

Shamanic Wisdom

Communicating With Trees

Trees are one of the most grounded and stable beings on the planet. Their roots reach deep into the earth to provide stability and to locate nutrients. Spending time with trees is one of the best ways to communicate with Earth Mother, especially if you are seeking balance.

Go to a natural place and pick up a fallen leaf. (Please don't pull a living leaf off a tree.) Sit or lie down and close your eyes. Holding the leaf, breathe deeply and relax. Ask the trees to grant you their strength, stability, balance and ancient wisdom; or ask a question, directing the question to all trees, through the leaf.

Then be receptive to feelings, to the first words you hear in your mind, to visualization, or to body sensations. This is your answer. Don't try to analyze the meaning of the answer until you are through. Analysis gets in the way of communicating with nature beings. Thank the Tree Spirits when you are through.

Communicating With Birds

When you find a feather on the ground, this is an invitation from the birds to communicate with them, for all the winged beings are messengers for the Great Spirit. Stop what you are doing, pick up the feather, hold it to your heart and ask the Bird Spirits for their wisdom or ask them to relay a prayer for you to the Creator or just ask a personal question. They are sure to answer you if you but listen with your heart.

We Are All Related

In a very short time you will discover you can communicate with any natural being. You will come to understand which beings to ask for specific assistance or insight as well. For example, you can attain greater steadfastness in your life by asking the stones to teach you about this virtue. Or you might ask the rain to teach you about nurturing or the evergreens about constancy. The possibilities are as boundless as nature Herself, and await your discovery. Just hold the stone or pine cone or rain water in your hand. Ask. Then listen.

If you wish to communicate with a natural being that is not present in your immediate surroundings (such as whales or polar bears), let an image of that being form within you. Hold the image of that being just as you held the pine cone or stone and proceed just as you did with them. You'll find this works best when done in a natural setting, too. And remember to thank these distant beings for talking with you just as you did those close by.

In a rather short time you will come to the place where getting in touch with nature beings isn't a matter of "doing exercises," but of spontaneous interaction—the kind of constant give and take that goes on among friends.

Another way to seek guidance from Earth Mother is to meditate each day on a being in nature and on how we might emulate that being in our daily lives. Ask yourself how you might learn from the plants, animals and minerals, in order to attain wisdom. For example, if you are spending a day thinking about Bear, you might look around at your own den and see how you can make it warm and safe, emotionally, just as Bear does with her den. Or when you need to be loyal, think of Wolf and let yourself be inspired by Wolf's loyalty. Or when you find yourself working too much, think of Otter; then go and play for a while.

As we go about our daily lives, we often wonder what is the best course of action in a given situation. At those times, we can stop for a moment and ask for guidance from Earth Mother, secure in the knowledge that She is a constant source of wisdom for Her children. There are many ways to seek this guidance, and this is basically what this book, and a shamanic path, is all about.

To make seeking guidance from nature work, you have to be very familiar with the ways of nature; for She has other important lessons to teach those who want to learn shamanic ways. As I said before, shamanic insights and abilities come from Earth Mother. So living as close to Her as you can is absolutely necessary to your evolution in shamanic awareness. After all, shamans among the primal people don't spend all their time journeying to the spirit world or conducting ceremonies. They gather food or make baskets or hunt like anyone else. This everyday contact with the natural world, this intimacy with the cycles of seasons and of birth, growth and death—these are the root sources of their shamanic powers. They function as shamans *because* they function as hunters and farmers, not in spite of it.

Even the most urban person can increase his or her interaction with the natural forces in meaningful ways. You can grow some of your own food by sprouting seeds in a jar or by growing some herbs in flowerpots on a windowsill. Larger plants can be raised in boxes or barrels on a balcony or patio. You can take responsibility for keeping a portion of a park free of litter. You can scatter wildflower seeds on roadside banks. You can take in strayed or wounded animals. You can observe how your own or other peoples' pets interact with the natural environment and learn from them how to be in nature. Again, the possibilities are too numerous to list them all. But if you start looking for the opportunities in your own situation, all kinds of exciting ways to become more closely involved with the natural world will open themselves to you. Any activity that draws us more deeply into natural forces such as growth, diversity, fostering, protecting and acting harmoniously will deepen our shamanic potential. No beginning is too small. No interaction with the cycles and dynamics of nature is insignificant.

Finally, keep these things in mind as you move to become a more intentional part of the great web of energy that is nature. Express your thanks to the natural beings when you are with them, whether sitting by a waterfall or feeding the birds or just standing in your own backyard.

Be with nature as often as you can. And take care to move lightly in nature, disturbing as little as possible and destroying nothing.

CHAPTER 2
THE GREAT MYSTERY

SACRED POWER

Shamanism is called a path of sacred power because on this path we learn to develop powers that are usually considered beyond human abilities. Our culture might call these psychic or magical powers. But these sacred powers are actually rooted in the natural world and are developed in conjunction with that world.

Although not everyone can or will want to be a shaman, everyone has some latent shamanic powers they can tap—far more, in fact, than they ever dreamed of, for shamanic wisdom and power are simply the wisdom and power of Earth Mother, and every child of Earth Mother is given some gift, some special power. Just as Eagle can see far, some people can see in a telepathic way. Just as Wolf is loyal, some people's medicine power is the ability to make many true friends. Just as Dolphin is wise, so some people are born with an inner knowing. And all of us have the potential to develop various shamanic powers, for these powers lie deep in the heart of everyone.

Those of us on a shamanic path draw our power and wisdom from the Earth, for this is an Earth religion. We embrace love of nature and closeness to Earth Mother as our spiritual path. We do not seek power as such. We seek communion and connection with nature—to spend time with the trees, waters, animals and birds, rocks, stars and flowers. We speak with all the animals, plants and minerals of this planet; and we hear with our hearts all that they say in return. We work for a close connection with Nature, for intimate communion with all creatures. So our goal is not power in and of itself but rather union. That is why we spend time outdoors, talking and listening, praying and meditating, picking up litter, planting seedlings or just being there. The closer our contact with nature, the more sacred power and wisdom are given us.

The essential thing you must realize here is that you do not set out to achieve shamanic power—you set out to achieve oneness and connection with nature; with our sacred Earth Mother. This connection inevitably leads to sacred power. The more you can communicate with and understand all of nature's wisdom, the more sacred power Earth Mother will grant you.

You cannot decide exactly what, when and where your power is given to you. This sacred power unfolds in us, gradually, as we commit ourselves more and more deeply to understanding, communicating with and acting on behalf of all living beings. It unfolds slowly over the seasons. You cannot grab it or rush it or push it. The Nature Spirits recognize our particular and individual talents,

The Great Mystery

inclinations and capacities. And in their own good time they decide which powers to share with us, the ones best suited to us. That is why one person becomes a healer, another a sacred dreamkeeper, another a rainbow warrior. That is why we cannot chose a particular expression of sacred power. It chooses us. All we can do is demonstrate our readiness to share in the powers of creation. And we demonstrate that readiness by dedicating our lives to stewarding and healing Earth Mother. The more firmly we dedicate ourselves to service of the Earth, therefore, the more we will be entrusted to share Earth Mother's many powers.

Although this book can teach you methods of acquiring medicine power, it is another thing to teach the love and reverence towards Earth Mother that is the most important element in gaining this power. If you go into nature often to revere Her and learn from Her, if you serve Her in mundane and spiritual ways, then the mystery power will be given to you.

Open your heart to Earth Mother, for She is now calling Her human children to return to Her ways. She is calling you to serve Her, love Her, be healed by Her and to be made whole and powerful.

Opening Your Heart To Earth Mother

Upon arising each day, go outside and put your hands over your heart. Pray to Earth Mother to open your heart to Her. Ask Her to help you get closer to Her in all ways. Ask that you might serve Her well.

Then let yourself become aware of your feelings. Let Her love bathe you in the healing wholeness of unconditional love. Then begin to speak to Earth Mother. Discuss or ask anything that comes to mind.

Now listen for an answer from Her. This answer might come from something you notice in nature; the way a bird calls, the way an insect behaves, the sound of the wind in the leaves. Or Her answer may come to you at the level of feelings, ideas or visualizations you may have.

When you are through communicating with your Mother, give Her thanks and go about your day with Her love and Her wisdom in your heart.

Earth Mother's Altar

Set up an altar inside your house dedicated to Earth Mother. Put a houseplant, a stone, pictures of nature or anything that links and connects you to Her, in one area. This might be a low table in front of which you can kneel or sit, or it might be just a window sill. You might place a dish of water, earth, a candle and a feather on Her altar to represent the four elements of earth, water, fire and air. Sit or kneel in front of Her altar each day and contemplate Earth Mother. Bring offerings and gifts to Her and place them on the altar as well—a piece of homemade bread, a crystal, or some other gifts to share with Her. Take care of Her altar, dust it, arrange it in a beautiful way; bring other lovely objects of nature to place upon it; let this caretaking represent your treatment of Earth Mother.

On this path, power isn't something we can get or hold; it is, rather, something shared with us, something which flows into us *because* we are connected with the source of power—creation itself.

The Great Mystery

So if we set out to *get* power, we are like those plants the heavy rains cause to spring up on stony ground. We may look good for awhile, but we won't last long because we have no roots. Yet whatever we do to root ourselves in Nature—to increase our love and understanding of Her—inevitably deepens our bond with Earth Mother and all beings. And we are given the capability to deepen our understanding and will to affirm life in even more powerful ways. Nature herself empowers us to grow in understanding and to serve the Creation.

We also increase our powers by sharing them. A strong, flowing stream can wear away the most solid rock and bring life over great distances. But when that same stream is dammed up, its energy turns inward and becomes stagnant. It is less wonderfully alive and it shares life with far fewer creatures. If we attempt to hoard our powers, then, we deny them, ourselves and the very reason those powers were shared with us in the first place. And we also put ourselves at risk. The living force of the stream always tries to break through the dam. And when it finds a weak point, it will burst through with frightening and destructive force.

That is why we always seek to share even further the powers that Nature shares with us. That is why we seek to act out our powers in ways that affirm and benefit all life, just as those powers have affirmed and benefited us. For we are like the channel or streambed for the flow of the universe's energy. We function best when the power can flow freely through us to do what it needs to do.

And it is not the streambed that determines the force or direction of the rushing water; it is the life energy of the waters. So we cannot say, for example, that we've done enough if we've spent some time meditating outdoors. The waters may want to carve a deeper channel, one that cuts into dreams and visions. Nor can we say that this direction or that is all that we will do. We may indeed send money to save the whales, but the powers of Nature may also push us toward spending all our free time planting trees.

You never know how walking a path of sacred power will affect you, but it will change your life in some profound ways. Nature Spirituality cannot be practiced on Sunday mornings only.

SEEING IN A SACRED MANNER

Shamans can "see" in ways not thought possible in our society. We, too, can discover our abilities to see in a sacred manner. In our culture we call this type of seeing "psychic ability" or "mystic vision." There are many ways to gain this special sight. We are all born with some psychic medicine powers, and we can develop others. A good way to begin is to discover our innate psychic abilities first and work on those—then later we can add other abilities less accessible to us.

It is important first to realize that there are many different ways to see in a sacred manner. You probably have not heard of some of them and never knew they existed, even if you have accidentally happened to experience one or more of them yourself. Listed below are some of the many ways of seeing in a sacred manner—but the list is much longer, for some people "see" in ways that no one else does. Remember, no one, not even the greatest of shamans, can do it all. Nevertheless, we all have certain proclivities and talents that we can develop.

Seeing Spirit Beings - The ability to see Nature Spirits, Angels, Extra-Terrestrials and so forth.

Astral Projection - The ability to leave the body behind while the soul travels through time and space, and then return again to the body.

Manifestation Medicine - Whether through prayer, visualization, affirmations, raising medicine power or some other means, the ability to manifest one's wishes and desires on the earth plane.

Weather Medicine - The ability to make it rain or otherwise influence the weather.

Perceiving Auras - The ability to see auras, to read a person's health through her aura and to affect her aura for the good.

Divination - The ability to know the future. To aid the process, many people use focusing systems such as I Ching, Tarot, crystal gazing and so forth. Others "know" through dreams or intuition.

Dowsing - The ability to sense the presence of water.

Healing Medicine - The ability to affect physical health through spirit means such as praying, laying on of hands, raising medicine power or working through animal spirit guardians.

Channeling - The ability to hear and even dialogue with Spirit Beings.

Lucid Dreaming - The ability consciously to affect our dreams.

Shamanic Wisdom

There are also many ways to "see" in a sacred manner that cannot be summed up in a simple phase and are not acknowledged at all in our society. Below is a partial list of them.

Keepers of the Ceremonies - These people have an innate ability to create rituals and ceremonies that speak to all people and that tap primal, archetypal wisdom and healing for those who participate in the ceremonies.
Peace Makers - These gentle souls see peace in every situation and exert a calming effect wherever they go.
Rainbow Warriors - These courageous people fight for truth, justice and the underdog. They are often environmental activists.
Ancient Wisdom Keepers - These folks know about the eternal truths of life and death and life after death.
Empaths - These people feel the pain and the joy of other beings and treat all life as if it were as important as their own. This is the most sacred seeing of all.

It is important for people from our culture to remember that anyone can develop a psychic or magical power, but it's not really sacred seeing if it is not accompanied by the realization that all life is related and the will to use these powers and seeings for the good.
We Americans keep confusing the psychic with the sacred. Having great psychic and magic abilities is not remarkable. Being empathic, kind, and life-protecting is. If you can blend them, then you can truly help yourself and all of life.
The best way to learn to see in a sacred manner is to

discover how you see best. Some people see from the heart, with their feelings. Others see from their eyes; they see auras and energy fields and even see the Nature Spirits in physical form. Others see by mentally hearing voices, words or ideas from the spirit world. Still others see with their body sensations, while some see in a way they can't describe. They just know it or feel it in their spirits. Anything that develops our intuition, creativity and imagination also develops sacred seeing.

Most books and teachers encourage their students and readers to "see" like they do. If the author is a visualizer, then to be a shaman you have to visualize. If the author is an emotionalizer, then you've got to see with your emotions. It is sad when emotionalizers try for years to "see" by visualizing, or when gifted vision seers exclusively try to get messages through body sensations.

When I or other authors lead you toward an inner vision quest, we say it that way because we are visualizers. You may go on an inner tasting, feeling, touching or hearing quest, or you may go within using some or all of these psychic senses.

People who are very visually oriented might find that seeing in a sacred manner literally means seeing Devas, Faeries, Elves and Nature Spirits. These are the Earth Spirits who share this planet with us, but who are invisible to most of us.

Seeing Earth Spirits

Go to a natural place bearing a gift for the Earth Spirits: perhaps a piece of fruit, a crystal or a few coins. Look for a natural opening such as a hole in the ground, a crevice in a stone or a hollow in a tree; these are faerie doors. Place your gift in or near the opening. Now sit or stand quietly in front of the opening and call to the nature folk, the little people, telling them you come as a friend. Then allow yourself to enter a meditative state, or simply sit quietly...If you are moved to sing or recite poetry, do this—for the Earth Spirits love song and rhyme—then sit quietly for a while. You might eventually see flickering, darting flashes of light out of the corners of your eyes. This is how the Earth Spirits first show themselves to us. Eventually you may see them in their actual forms.

Some people who are visually oriented might find that they can see spirit beings of the celestial realms such as angels, extra-terrestrials and various other heavenly deities.

Others might find that they can close their eyes and mentally visualize very clearly and vividly—so vividly it is as if it really happens. Talented visualizers can manifest reality by continual visual affirmative exercises.

People who are very communicative with other people, those whose hearts, minds and mouths are always open, might well find that communication is their shamanic birthright as well. For example, channeling might be their forte. They might receive messages from or dialogue with higher beings, Nature Spirits, deities and other beings from the Spirit World.

People who are naturally dreamy and vague in the waking state may be very talented in the dreamtime. They might develop the ability to have medicine dreams, gain great insight and wisdom from their dreams, meet with spirit beings in the dreamtime and become lucid dreamers.

The Great Mystery

Those who are very kindhearted and empathic might find that they can connect at a heart level with animals, plants and minerals and tap the great ancient healing wisdom of all the nature beings through knowledge of the heart.

The first step in developing shamanic seeing, then, is to know yourself. Are you a visualizer, an emotionalizer, or a verbalizer? Or do you access the world through bodily sensations? People who do that can learn to feel other people's bodily sensations. They might become healers.

To determine whether you are a visualizer, an emotionalizer, a verbalizer or kinesthetic (one who feels) and to determine which is your strongest or weakest area, do this exercise:

Accessing Sacred Seeing

Close your eyes and see yourself walking towards your mailbox. Inside you find an envelope. You open it and see that someone has given you a million dollars. You feel good, you feel happy.

Let yourself examine the moment. Did you experience the excitement of this imaginary happening in your real-world body? Did you see yourself walking to the mailbox? Could you clearly see the day's sunlight flooding the picture? Did you notice what you were wearing? Were the colors bright and vibrant? Did you feel your clothes on your body or the feel of the envelope in your hands?

Now close your eyes and imagine a ripe juicy peach. You lift the peach in your hand and feel its weight, the soft fuzz on its skin. Did you clearly see its colors, the reds and yellows and oranges. Gently press the peach with your

23

*fingertips. Can you feel it give slightly? Now take a bite out
of it and imagine its taste in your mouth. Did you feel its
sweetness fill your mouth? Did you feel the subtle changes
in texture as you chewed? Did you tasted the juice on your
lips, smell its aroma waft to your nose?*

*Now close your eyes again and hear your parents
speaking to you. They are saying something that makes you
feel a certain way, maybe good, maybe bad. Did you
actually hear their voice in your mind? How did it make you
feel?*

Hopefully, the above exercise will help you determine the way or ways that you can best access your sacred
sight. Most people are especially gifted in one or two areas;
it is rare to respond equally well to all of them.

There are so many different ways of "seeing" that
you may have a way all your own, one not described or
taught anywhere else. You may just have to develop it
yourself. If this is the case, you shouldn't feel alone and
isolated, but honored that you have been singled out for a
unique gift.

In all my years of teaching shamanic seeing to
students I've noticed that you can divide sacred seeing into
certain categories which I've come to call the Sunlight
Vision, the Moonlight Vision, The Starlight Vision, and the
Earthlight Vision. I find that we gravitate naturally to one
of these ways more than to the others. We were all born
with a proclivity to see best with one of these visions,
sometimes two, but we can develop our ability to see with
any of them if we want to. Begin with the type of vision that
you achieve most easily. Soon you can branch out and

incorporate any of the others that you wish.

Moonlight Vision

The Moonlight Vision is seen most readily by those who identify with the feminine, with gentleness, nurturing and kindness. People who access this vision aren't interested in power, but in connectedness, in oneness. The Moonlight Vision is often accessed by the dreamy, gentle, soft, empathic soul. When this tender vision is frustrated and twisted, it can turn into eccentricity, weakness, depression, self-destructiveness and cowardice.

The animals who teach us to see with the Moonlight Vision and stay on a positive path with it include all cats other than Lion, and Owl.

It is best to do the following exercise at various moon phases, for each time you do it you will receive the gift of Moonlight Vision appropriate for that phase of the moon.

Learning To See With Moonlight Vision

Go out on a clear night and lie down under the moon. Breathe deeply. When you feel centered and calm, pray to the moon to awaken your Moonlight Vision. Address the moon for the phase she is in. If it is a full moon, for instance, say "Mother, grant me Moonlight Vision that I may see abundantly." Or if it is a new moon, say "Corn Maiden, grant me Moonlight Vision, that I may see in a new way." Or if it's a dark moon, say "Grandmother, grant me Moonlight Vision, that I may see with ancient wisdom." Then just gaze at the moon and accept the moonlight into yourself. Let it bathe you and enter you and transform you.

I highly recommend moon gazing for developing the moonlight vision. Any time you can, lie down and gaze at Her. She will re-infuse you with the power to see with Her vision. While you are doing this, you can also talk to Her and She will answer you in some manner. To see with the Moonlight Vision, you must have a relationship with the moon.

Dancing in the Moonlight Vision into yourself is another alternative. Go out under the moon and dance for Her and with Her. Praise Her and love Her. When you are done, gaze at Her and let the Moonlight Vision enter you. You might find that your dance is very different each time, depending on the moon phase.

If you are owned by a cat, your cat can teach you much about forming a relationship with the moon. Since Cat and Moon are close kin and clan related, cats see with Moonlight Vision better than any other being on earth. And that is also why their eyes change phases just as Moon does.

If you do not have a cat companion, then you might ask Cat Spirit to help you see with the Moonlight Vision. But first gift cat by helping a stray cat, helping an institution that cares for cats, or sending money to help the big cats in the jungles. By doing this you become attuned to Cat. There is no other Nature Spirit as *quid pro quo* as Cat. You must give to Cat to get anything back. Nor is there any other Nature Spirit that can teach humans as much about seeing with the Moonlight Vision. (Owl knows as much as Cat, but doesn't teach humans as often.) That is why Cat is living with humans now: to teach us their mysterious,

26

moonlit wisdom.

After you have gifted Cat you can invoke cat's power by ritually decorating yourself as Cat, moving as Cat, as much as possible becoming Cat. This honors Cat and also demonstrates to her that you are serious in your intentions. Your "costume" could be as simple as drawing a set of whiskers on your face with an eyebrow pencil. Also put on a moon symbol of some kind that shows Cat what you are trying to achieve. Cut a crescent moon out of paper and place it on your body. Then go under the moon and become Cat. Walk, move, sound, feel and be as Cat. Ask Cat to enter you and to teach you all you need to know to be one with Moon.

Emulate cats in all ways and you will better see with Moonlight Vision. For example, cats cleanse all the time. If you smudge and cleanse on a sacred level, you will make a sacred space for the Moonlight Vision to shine within you. Cats like to go out at night, and live much of their life beneath the moon. If you go out more at night, in quiet, wild places under the moon, you will invite the Moonlight Vision in.

Earthlight Vision

The Earthlight Vision is seen by those who so love nature that it is like a drug to them. Their hearts are one with all of nature. They go to wild and natural places at every opportunity and even if they live in a large urban area they always manage to find a bit of earth to visit, a few plants to care for, an animal to befriend. These people are the ones with a great indoor garden and eight stray cats even if they live in a highrise apartment in the middle of Manhattan.

The Earthlight Vision allows us eventually to see or feel or hear the Nature Spirits, the Devas, the elfin folk and the faeries that inhabit and watch over field and forest. Those who most easily see with the Earthlight Vision must be in nature often. For it is there, in their true home, that their spirits will be be able to perceive the knowledge and find the vision that is their true birthright. Although these people often have an elfin sense of humor, they are usually very grounded people, with their feet firmly planted on the earth they love so well.

Needless to say, you can't really walk a shamanic path if you don't have at least a little bit of the Earthlight Vision, so if you are wondering which vision you would like to develop first, perhaps here would be a good place to start.

Developing Earthlight Vision

Go out into nature, preferably a place where you can spend some time alone without being disturbed by other people. Begin to empty your logical mind by chanting, singing, gently dancing, or perhaps shaking a rattle. Do not try to intentionally do anything, merely enjoy and observe the beauty and peace that is around you.

At some point you will notice something calling to you: a pebble, a twig, a leaf, a feather, a shell...Pick it up, sit or lie down and become quiet. Put the object over your heart, close your eyes, and make a request or ask a question. For instance, if you have picked up a twig, you might ask for communication with the Tree Spirits. If you have picked up

The Great Mystery

a feather you might ask for more freedom in your life. After you have asked your question, simply wait patiently until you feel, see, hear or think something that seems to be significant to you. It may be an emotion, an idea, the appearace of a particular animal or some other sign from nature.

Try not to analyze what is happening. This is not an intellectual exercise but an attempt to communicate in a non-intellectual way with non-verbal entities. Analyzing will inhibit and perhaps stop the process. When you are done, then you can think about what happened and what it meant.

The more you are in nature without distractions—without music, books, or others to talk to—the more the Earthlight Vision will grow strong in you. The more you open your heart to the beings of nature, the wider Earth Mother will open your eyes and heart to the Earthlight Vision.

Sunlight Vision

Sunlight Vision is the worldview that most of us were consciously and unconsciously taught as children. Of course, it is never called by that name. Nevertheless, whenever anyone with the mindset of the predominate culture, in both the Eastern and Western traditions, addresses spiritual matters it is usually evident that they have looked at their subject using the Sunlight Vision. The Sunlight Vision is often, but not always, a male way of seeing. It is the hunter's sacred sight, and uses the head rather than the heart. Eagle and Lion are the foremost teachers of the Sunlight Vision.

Because Sunlight Vision is a transcendental way of seeing, most of the Eastern, Christian, and modern techniques for engaging the right brain will open up the Sunlight Vision. Since the mainstream culture explores this aspect of spiritualiy so thoroughly I will not go into it extensively here, but I will point out that the Sunlight Vision is associated with the warrior/hunter—one who possesses abundant courage, aggressiveness, valor, and is protective of those he loves. The Sunlight Seer possesses and respects logical and analytical ability, as well as transcendence of and sometimes dominance over the earth plane and often perceives a spiritual path as an accumulation of power. This way of seeing, when distorted or perverted, can become cold, impersonal, cruel, meanspirited and life-destroying.

If you want to explore the Sunlight Vision, go into any metaphysical bookstore and ask for books on developing psychic powers and abilities. Actually, most of the books there on any subject will be slanted heavily towards sacred seeing with the Sunlight Vision. Almost every modern westerner who currently addresses inner seeing approaches it as if the Sunlight Vision were the only sacred sight. This is easily understood in a male-dominated culture, but we should always keep in mind that reality—mundane, metaphysical, and psychic—can be perceived in ways other than this limited viewpoint.

The Great Mystery

The Starlight Vision

The Starlight Vision is a combination of all the other sacred ways of seeing. It is a mystical vision of cosmic consciousness. Those who can see with this vision tap into the limitless vastness of the universe and of the soul. Many primal cultures and not a few contemporary authors believe that we were originally seeded here on earth from the stars. All matter on earth comes from a star that exploded, hurling itself through time and space till it eventually condensed into this planet. So we are stardust, drifting through the cosmos, stopping to dance with the sun for a few billion years before moving on to as yet unborn universes. Our spirits were forged in the heat, the light and the passion of the ancient heavens. All living beings on earth are star children, and the Starlight Vision is the birthright of every one of us.

Seeing with the Starlight Vision means seeing the whole, the entirety, the gestalt—without limitations of time or space. Seeing in this manner is conducive to telepathy, clairvoyance, divination and so forth. It is also conducive to intuiting and "knowing" deep cosmic wisdom.

Developing Starlight Vision

On a clear night, lie down under the stars. As you gaze at the sky, let your attention be drawn to one particular star. As you gaze at this star, you will notice that it seems to be shining just for you. Meditate on the light, and feel the starlight enter you through your eyes. Then close your eyes and breathe in deeply. Feel the starlight begin to fill you. As the light overflows, feel the starlight pour out of your

31

heart and surround the earth. Feel your awareness expand-
ing with the light...Now feel the light expand to cover this
solar system, then the galaxy, then the universe and sense
your awareness expanding with the starlight.

Simply gazing at the stars often, while asking to be
granted starlight vision will also open up our innate abilities
to "see" in this way. It is impossible to look up at the night
sky on a clear night and behold the layers of stars, the bright
span of the Milky Way, without being awed by the incom-
prehensible vastness of creation. The Starlight Vision is
unique in its ability to teach us that the only limits are those
we have imposed on ourselves.

SACRED IMAGINATION

After you've had your first interactions with the spirit
realm, you may find yourself wondering if your experience
was "real" or "just my imagination." This is not unusual
at all. Indeed, most of my beginning students ask the same
kinds of questions and experience similar doubts. This is an
important issue and one that must be faced if you're going
to walk the shamanic path for very long.

Mainstream culture tends to dismiss experiences
that go beyond the world of the senses as figments of our
imaginations. But other cultures, those that value shamanism and the nuances of spiritual experiences, hold the
imagination as sacred. Think of what Joan of Arc said when
her accusers told her that her voices and visions were "just
your imagination." She replied, "God speaks to us through
our imagination."

The Great Mystery

The spirit world speaks to us through our imaginations, through our visualizations and visions, through feelings in our hearts, through words we hear in our minds, through dreams, symbols and signs. So it's important that we learn to trust our imaginations and the ways of knowing that the imagination opens to us. Far from being apologetic and doubtful about such experiences, we must learn to honor and embrace them. These are the means, the central and sacred means, by which the worlds of nature and spirit communicate with us. In a similar way, whenever you are in nature, any thoughts, feelings or impressions you get are the way the Nature Spirits communicate with you.

Just as the spirit realm speaks to us through our imaginations, so do we communicate with spirit the same way. Therefore, rituals, ceremonies and medicine circles are most powerful if they are self-created or group-created with as much imagination as possible. That is why these ceremonies are often beautiful. But they can also be filled with laughter and spontaneity as well. That is why we chant, dance, move, speak and pray with every part of ourselves. That is why these rituals are filled with drama and poetry. We do these things so that every part of our imaginations can speak to spirit and listen to spirit in return.

The main difference between a shaman and an ordinary person is that a shaman takes very seriously all information received through imagination. When we honor such experiences, we also distinguish ourselves from those who reject this plane of reality. We set ourselves firmly on the shamanic path.

Whenever you happen to find yourself about to dismiss some feeling, impression or thought as "just my imagination," stop for a moment. Consider whether Earth Mother, the Nature Spirits or other spirit beings might in fact be breaking through to you at that time and in that way.

CHAPTER 3
IN A SACRED MANNER

GIFTING, GIVING THANKS, GIVING BACK

On the shamanic path we constantly experience the healing and blessings Earth Mother showers on Her children. We always give back to life, to nature and to the earth, for Earth Mother has given us the gift of life. As we walk the shamanic path, we are also given great gifts of power and healing by Earth Mother. We therefore also experience the need to show our gratitude and to offer something to Her in return. In the process of doing so, our lives will be blessed and our Earth will be healed. In learning to have a giving heart, we ourselves receive the greatest gift.

And it is good for us to feel the need to give thanks, to give back. There's something in the human heart that needs to feel thankful, or else we become cynical and embittered. Our spirits begin to shrink and we lose medicine power. But feeling grateful and giving back to life opens and expands our spirits, allowing us to grow and blossom and unfold our shamanic powers. By giving back we join ourselves with the great act of giving which is the life force of nature and the universe.

This endless flow of giving, receiving and giving again produces harmony and balance in nature, where it is easy to observe. The oaks give their leaves to the earth, feeding the earthworms and microorganisms that in turn feed the soil that in turn feeds the oak again. And the growing oak shelters birds and feeds the squirrels. It is not natural, then, to think only of receiving. That creates imbalance and leaves our spirits shriveled and starved.

To enter the balanced flow of receiving and giving, we must first learn how to accept gifts, large or small, with a thankful heart. Each breath, each day, each change in season or weather is a gift from Earth Mother. So we learn to thank Her often for the basics of our lives. Doing so reminds us of how much we receive from our sacred Earth Mother and puts us in a proper relationship with Her—a relationship of reverence and thankfulness. So as you awaken, if your first conscious thought is a word of thanks for the gift of another day of life, this will set the tone for the rest of the day. Your day will unfold in gladness and gratitude. And when we eat, we remember in thanks the plants and animals that gave their life energies to sustain our own.

We learn to express our thanks out loud for the beauty we encounter in nature, for the wind and sun and moon and stars. Simply speak from your heart. For example, the first time you see the sun each day you might say something like, "Sun Father, I give thanks for your life-giving warmth." On a cloudy day you might say, "Thank you clouds, for the rain that refreshes the earth." Or the first time you feel the breeze each day you might say something like, "Wind Spirits, thank you for carrying the seeds to their new homes." Feeling and expressing our gratitude for every aspect of our lives is like food to our spirits.

Only in the natural climate of gratitude and thankfulness can our spirits flourish. Yet some of us find it hard to feel thankful in our hearts. We modern westerners were not raised in a culture that gives thanks. Because we were raised in a culture that takes and takes in a greedy frenzy and then feels nothing but the need to take more, some of us find it difficult to have genuine feelings of thankfulness in our hearts. No matter. Just start giving thanks out loud, and the very process of speaking the thanks all day long will awaken your spirit and open your heart. Saying our thanks out loud (or singing them or dancing them) stirs our souls and makes them even more capable of gratitude—and of the next step, giving back.

When our hearts and spirits fill with gratitude for all of nature's gifts, they want to overflow into action. You reach the place where words are not enough by themselves. So maybe having given thanks, for example, because you are about to enjoy a cool drink of spring water, you give some of that water back to the earth from which it came by splashing a bit onto a tuft of grass or sprig of flowers. Or suppose you notice that a beach has been trashed. You give back by picking up the trash and giving the gift of unspoiled beauty to others. Perhaps there are stray animals in your neighborhood. You give back by doing all you can to share your gifts with them. Maybe you will be moved to join an active environmental protection group or plant seedlings on a roadside bank to help hold the soil. In the cold of winter, you might put food out for the birds, squirrels and other wildlife in your area. Remember (and this is the one of the most important things to realize in order to walk a shamanic path), you must not take nature's gifts and tap nature's power for yourself and then watch as nature suffers and is destroyed around you. Earth Mother's gifts are boundless, but humankind has so taken advantage of Her generosity that Her need for stewarding and protection are also great at this time. Opportunities to give back are all around you. You have only to open yourself, in gratitude, and the way you can give back will be shown you.

Prayers and rituals also provide a means of giving back. At the spiritual level you share the energies you have been given, especially to beings in need of such help, like species threatened with extinction or streams polluted by human activity. This can be as simple as visualizing and praying that the streams run clean and clear again—or as complex as going to a polluted stream and spending the day praying, chanting, visualizing and sending the Water Spirits of that place love and healing in every way you can. There are many Earth-healing, nature-protecting rituals and energy workings presented in this book to help you to help Earth Mother.

Also, when you pray to the Nature Spirits for something, it is good to gift them first. For instance, you could pray to the Bird Spirits if you are seeking freedom or the ability to soar in some way. Before you pray, you might toss bird seed upon the ground. Or you might pray to the Oak Spirits for strength, stability and longevity. Before you make your prayer, you might gift one oak tree, the representative of all oaks, with a drink of water.

Whenever you give back, whether in ritual or in concrete action, you complete the cycle by again giving thanks. After all, even the ability and energy to give back is itself a gift of our sacred Earth Mother!

SMUDGING, CLEANSING AND PURIFICATION

All spiritual paths have rituals of cleansing and purification. Smoke smudging is the most ancient and is also the most popular neo-shamanic way to purify our thoughts, our feelings and our spirits.

Just getting through our day-to-day life can cause unwanted energies to find a place in our hearts—the frustrations and petty jealousies we as humans are prone to. After all, who among us does not have negative thoughts and feelings from time to time? So we find it necessary to cleanse ourselves from time to time, and most especially before we attempt to work with any medicine powers.

Our green brothers and sisters, the plants, have the power to clear our hearts and minds. For the green plants of Earth Mother are filled with love and good will toward all life. That is why, when we go to a natural place, we feel refreshed, why our spirits are healed and cleansed. So we bathe ourselves in the smoke from the plants to purify ourselves, to refresh and cleanse ourselves ritually.

At its simplest, smudging means setting fire to some dried and fragrant plant material, extinguishing the flame and moving the still smoking material around your body or around an object you wish to cleanse.

Smudging restores balance and harmony through the transforming energy of fire and the purifying essence of a plant. Its physical processes, though external, mirror internal or spiritual processes of balancing and restoring to harmony. The plants used most commomly for smudging are cedar, sweetgrass and the sages, for they are thought to be particularly cleansing. These herbs can be gathered wild or obtained in a health food store or in some metaphysical bookstores. Some people use organically-grown dried mint, or spearmint tea right from a tea bag, or other cleansing herbs as smudge material. Still others gather leaves or evergreen needles that happen to be available where they live. Whatever you smudge with, make sure it is non-toxic, because you cannot help inhaling some of the smoke as you bathe your body with the smoke.

The simplest way to smudge involves using an incense stick. Cedar and pine incense are readily available. However, if you want to smudge with loose material, put a small amount of the dried plant material that you've chosen in a small pile in any fireproof container. Touch the pile here and there with a match until you get the whole thing aflame. You will probably have to work at this a little, for you are lighting a tiny fire and the same principles of lighting logs applies in miniature here. You must set fire to a small section on the bottom, and then add a little more material on top to get a small flame going. The very process of building your tiny fire is part of the cleansing ritual and has a focusing effect that links you to the primal experience of building a fire. When the little flame is going, stare into it and let your mind capture, for a moment, the awesome and hypnotizing effect of Fire. Then blow out all the flame at once. Lots of smoke will rise from the glowing dried plant material. At this point, all you need to do is lean over the smoking container and let the smoke flow over you. Or you can use your hands or a feather or a fan of branches to brush the smoke around you. Alternatively, you can pick up the whole container (being careful not to burn your fingers) and move it around your body or around the objects you are smudging.

No matter how you choose to bathe yourself in the smoke, you will probably want to make a short prayer, mentally or aloud, as you do so. Many people ask the spirits of the particular plant they are burning to purify them. For example, "Spirits of Cedar, may I be cleansed of negative thoughts and feelings. May my heart be made pure again that I might walk in balance and harmony." It is, of course, best if your prayer comes from your heart. And it can also be very specific if that is appropriate. For example, "Spirits of Sage, cleanse me of anger towards my husband." People also commonly ask to be cleansed of fears, worries, doubts, meanness, selfishness and so forth as they smudge themselves.

All of the above can be done on a larger scale, outdoors, with a campfire. But whether you use an incense stick or a bonfire to smudge, do it safely.

In addition to smudging ourselves, we can also smudge our living and working spaces, our gardens, our cars, our tools, our ritual objects, our jewelry, and so on. We do these things by passing the smoke around larger objects or by holding smaller ones over the smoke, asking for cleansing while this is being done.

We can also smudge each other in the same way that we smudge ourselves. People doing this for each other will often pray aloud for the person being smudged.

Smudging is also a common shamanic way to purify ourselves ritually at the beginning of a medicine wheel or at any other time we raise medicine power.

Smudging is a way of regaining, at least for awhile, the balance and natural sense of proportion we brought with us into this existence. It is an action both profoundly simple and simply profound.

There are, of course, other ways to purify our spirits with the help of nature. We can purify ourselves by interacting with any number of nature beings in our own intuitive ways. Water is very cleansing, and we can sprinkle some on ourselves while asking the Water Spirits to wash away fears and negativity. We can brush off unwanted energies with a feather or a leaf, or we can visualize white light entering our body, heart and spirit as we pray for purification. When we stand in a breeze, we can ask the Wind Spirits to blow away any general or specific negativity, and so forth.

All nature is purifying in its own way; and as you interact more and more with Her, you can find spontaneous situations that lend themselves to cleansing your heart and spirit.

PROTECTION

We live in a society that produces many harmful and negative energies—air and noise pollution, overcrowding, assaults on the environment and the general stresses of everyday living in a modern, urban culture. Another kind of stress, and one I consider as devastating, is the lack of spiritual connectedness that would allow us to deal with and remedy these problems.

Spirit pouches or medicine bags are a simple yet important shamanic approach to help us reconnect ourselves to our spiritual roots in nature and protect ourselves as well. You can make a spirit pouch to wear on your person, keep in your car or house or carry with you in your pocket or briefcase. You can make the pouch any size you want, of any material you find appropriate, or you can purchase one ready-made. But the pouch is less important than what you put in it—objects from nature associated with the powers of protection.

Fill your spirit pouch with herbs, stones and other natural things that have protective powers. For example, porcupine quills, a turtle's shell or a sea shell are associated with protection because that is their natural function. (Obtain things like this *after* the porcupine, turtle or sea creature has died naturally!) Various shamanic cultures have come to associate particular minerals (quartz crystals, agate and turquoise are examples) with protection. Other cultures designate special trees (e.g., oak trees) or animals (e.g., the she-bear) as being especially protective. And although learning the details of such traditional beliefs and practices are useful (find at the end of this section a list of protective nature beings), you will probably find that your greatest

Shamanic Wisdom

natural protectors are the nature beings you have befriended and attempted to protect. After all, the balance of giving, receiving, forming relationships and creating allies with the natural world is what shamanism is all about.
Begin collecting power objects of nature beings whom you have helped or protected. If you work to stop acid rain, the fir trees you have fought for would be represented in your spirit pouch. Simply collect a piece of twig or a leaf from the ground (do not cut or harm the tree) and put it in your medicine bag. A tuft of cat hair tucked into your pouch would represent all the stray animals you have taken in or helped to save from destruction in an animal pound or laboratory. A small statuette, medallion, drawing or picture of mountains, the desert, or of particular plants and animals will lend you the protective powers of these entities—especially if you have befriended them and worked for their preservation.
As you collect these power objects, remind the Tree Spirits or the Cat Spirits, for example, that you have protected them and ask for their protection in return. Keep you medicine bag with you always. Take the power objects out often to re-infuse them with your prayers for protection.
Another protective gift from nature is the circle. The circle suggests not only the defensive perimeter used by some herd animals but the protective powers of the sacred circle or medicine wheel. We can make a protective circle anytime and anyplace, temporarily or permanently. We can visualize a circle around ourselves whenever we feel the need of spirit protection. I visualize a circle of oak trees around myself as I ask the Oak Spirits for protection. Others visualize a ring of crystals, or fire, or water, or white

light or any nature being that is protective to them. The circle can be small enough to include only yourself or large enough to embrace the cosmos. It can embrace your house, your town, the earth or the entire world. We can also draw a circle on the ground with a stick, enter that circle and pray for protection. Even drawing an invisible circle in the air or an invisible circle on the ground is viewed as protective. To be especially protective, the circle is drawn clockwise, or sunwise, for this is the direction of good luck or increasing abundance and energy.

Shielding is another form of protection, one in which we invite our allies in nature and the spirit world to block us from any energy we don't want. So if you perceive that someone bears you ill will or wishes you bad luck out of envy or jealousy, for example, you can ask your natural allies to stand between you and the source of those negative feelings, to deflect those expressions of ill will away from you, to return them to their source. (You can visualize your guardian animal, plant or mineral actually doing this.)

Whenever you have occasion to use one of these forms of protection, you will be aware that you have encountered negative energy. This is also an appropriate time to make use of one of the means of cleansing that we talked about earlier in this chapter. And, as always when nature spirits have come to your assistance, give them the thanks they're due.

Finally, I must reiterate that the more you protect nature and the nature beings, the more protection you will receive.

NATURE BEINGS ASSOCIATED WITH PROTECTION

Animals

All mother animals, especially She-Bear, Wolf, Elephant, Meercat(a relative of the Mongoose clan), Dog, Fox, Coyote, Dolphin, Skunk, Beaver, Porcupine, Turtle, Badger, all creatures with shells. Any animal that you have helped or protected.

Plants

(The plants on this list are not necessarily safe or good to eat).

Cedar, Gardenia, Geranium, Lemon, Myrrh, Rosemary, Spearmint, Garlic, Frankincense. All trees, especially Oak. Any plant that you have helped and protected.

Minerals

Agate, Alexandrite, Citrine, Coral, Crystal Cluster, Flint, Fluorite, Labradorite, Jet, Malachite, Quartz Crystal, Sard, Sardonyx, Tiger's Eye, Turquoise. Any stone from a natural place that you have helped and protected.

CHAPTER 4
EARTH ECSTASY

FINDING YOUR SACRED CLAN NAME

When you begin to pay attention to the natural world and to spend as much time as you can among the various beings in nature, you may begin to notice that one or two beings in particular start showing up almost everywhere in your life. You may find, by word, by symbol or by knowledge of the heart, that you are accepted as a clan member by these beings. For example, you might suddenly begin finding lots of crow feathers in your walks, or people might begin to give you a particular kind of stone, or you may find that a particular kind of plant presents itself wherever you go. Blue Jay might appear in your yard daily, or you might see Deer whenever you go into nature. Since plants can't move, one of the ways they let you know that you are a clan member is if you keep finding yourself living near a certain type of plant, no matter where you move. For example, sometimes you may live where pine trees are

47

common and sometimes not. But wherever you are attracted to locate your home, you find at least one pine nearby. The pines are calling you. Start listening.

Such occurrences are not coincidences; more likely, they are invitations from the animal, plant or mineral clans for you to form a special relationship with one or more members of these clans. You may be invited to join their clan and take their name as your sacred name.

For example, I was invited to join the Dolphin clan many years ago when I lived on an island off the coast of Florida. I was very isolated and lonely at this time. One day, as I was walking on the beach, I noticed two dolphins swimming close to shore and keeping up with me whenever I walked. When I sat down near the edge of the water, they swam in as close as they could. I cleared my mind and opened my heart. The unconditional love that poured into me from them was almost overwhelming. I sat on the beach, cried, laughed, and was healed on many levels by their love. Then one of the dolphins spoke to me with words I heard in my mind and said, "You do not have to be lonely. We will meet you here often. You will be a member of our clan, and you may bear the clan name of Dolphin." I answered back that I was honored, but I didn't think I could live up to the love and wisdom that came with this name. The dolphin responded, "Then you will have something to strive for." After that, they came often and we communicated. They taught me many things. This is why my name is Dolfyn and why Dolphin is my clan.

Whenever you notice some animal, plant or stone presenting itself to you in a particularly insistent way, pay close attention. Stop what you are doing, clear your mind and open your spirit to whatever that being wants to communicate to you. This being is trying to tell you something. See if you get a visualization, some words entering your mind, bodily sensations or feelings in your heart. Or they may communicate in ways you can't quite define. They may have an important lesson for you to learn at that moment. And once you have taken that lesson to heart, the frequency and/or intensity of their presence my return to normal. Or you may discover that the crows or the stones or the wild strawberries are inviting you to share a more long-term relationship.

After you have started to communicate with that being frequently, you may find that its name fits you. Should you decide to take that name for your own, you are acknowledging the companionship, help and power of that being and joining its energy to your own. For example, if by this process your sacred name becomes "Oak," you will begin receiving some of the powers, attributes and wisdom of Oak: stability, longevity and groundedness. If your sacred name is Horse you will begin to receive attributes like strength, endurance, power and grace.

There are many other ways to acquire a sacred name. We do not necessarily have to belong to the clan first, before we can have a sacred name. Some people take on a sacred name of a being in nature that they especially love, honor and respect. Eventually they find that they are invited into the clan of that being, by virtue of their emulation, honor and love for that nature clan. Others find that their sacred name comes in a dream or vision. Still others are named by humans. For example, a friend of mine was told by many people that she had a cat-like energy. She took on the name Cat, and it was right for her. Some people find that their sacred name is not necessarily a being of nature, but is descriptive of their spirit, while others find their name is a combination of both. For example, I know a blithe spirit whose name is Laughing Crow. Finally, some people find that their sacred name changes as they grow and develop. For example, another friend was Eagle in the glory of her youth, then, in the wisdom of middle age, her sacred name became Owl. Stay open to this process of growth and change. However, even if you are inspired to discard an old name for a more appropriate one at a certain stage of life, you still are a member of the old clan, as well as the new one.

Some people say that they have never experienced an invitation from any clan in nature. That may be, but it seems unlikely. Often these invitations are made in very subtle ways or are made by nature beings not often considered important by modern westerners. Stay open to all possibilities. Although it is more likely you'll be invited by nature beings you interact with frequently, like cats or birds, than beings you've seen only on T.V., like Grizzly or Wolf, it is possible to be invited to join these clans as well— especially if you have helped or given to this clan in some way. For example, if you have sent money to an organization to counteract the extinction of wolves, Wolf might come to you often in the dreamtime, inviting you to join her clan. Then you might take on the name Wolf.

Remember that all beings have special powers, not just those we think of as awe-inspiring or significant. If the sparrows want to love you, heal you or accept you into their clan, don't wait for a "better" offer from a Bengal tiger. You could wind up having a very lonely life!

Earth Ecstasy

When you join a clan and accept the sacred name that goes with it, you also accept special obligations to the family of creatures that bears your name. If you are Blue Bird, you will look after Blue Bird habitats and fight the use of pesticides which threaten them. If you are Willow, you will do all you can to make sure your family multiplies.

Once you've accepted a sacred name in this way, you have a lifelong connection with and obligation toward that clan, even if you change your sacred name or add others. But if you "live up to your name," you will find your life immeasurably enriched and empowered.

RHYTHM AND DANCE

All that is is in motion. Creation, far from being a series of objects, is an unimaginably complex dance comprised of innumerable interlocking motions and processes— from the unseen orbits of atoms to the swinging courses of the planets and stars. We know this with our heads. But, more importantly, our blood knows it. Our breath and hearts pulse to universal rhythms; our bodies, being mostly water, respond to the tidal pulls of the moon; the neurons in our brain pulse with their own dance of electric currents. We dance as grasses in the wind or seaweed in the tide. Our growth, maturity and decline echo the same rhythms of the annual cycles of green growing things and even the slower, more stately cycles that create and destroy mountains and river deltas. Our flowing flows into the Great Flow of all beings.

We move our awareness into these harmonies when

51

we go to some natural place and simply note our interior rhythms and the rhythms around us. We hear the cicadas and feel our blood's pulse. We tune our breathing to a bird song or the wash of the surf. We move our limbs to the movement of shadows on the grasses. We join the dance. We become the dance.

To join rhythmically in the movement of the creation allows us to experience the universal energies directly. That is why, in shamanic rituals, medicine wheels and ceremonies, we use chants, drums, rattles, dance, hand clapping and other activities which create a group pulse. Rhythm gets us in touch with the inner child and lifts up our spirits. When we are in group medicine wheels or other shamanic rituals, it is good to keep up a soft rhythm even when someone is speaking. We can beat a drum, clap our hands, pound the ground, shake a rattle, hit two sticks or stones together or use whatever is at hand to make rhythm. The rhythm stops us from intellectualizing and keeps us from rambling. The rhythm keeps us on the beat, literally and figuratively, and helps us to think, act and speak in a sacred manner.

In rhythmic movement we honor our bodies and move into the depths of our own sensuality. Rhythm gets us in touch with our bodies. If we ignore or deny our body's need for joyous and sensual expression through rhythm, we then also ignore and deny Earth Mother's joy, sensuality and rhythmic expression. As we learn to honor our sacred bodies, we learn to honor the sacred Earth herself. Our living bodies unite with Her living body.

Rhythmic expression and movement allows us to make strong prayers because in such expression we help shape the energies of life itself. In such expression we mingle our prayers and intentions with the powerful flow of universal life energy. Praise and celebration of life are also expressed through rhythm and dance. And since rhythm and movement raise energy, it is one of the most effective ways to raise medicine power. Our dancing brings the mystery power from the universe into our bodies and transforms that energy with rhythm and dance.

In our shamanic rituals and ceremonies "dance" does not necessarily mean a choreographed pattern of movement. It can mean the spontaneous celebration of life through movement, a direct experience of and interaction with the universe via the body. It need not be professional looking or even graceful, for if it comes from the heart it will be a beautiful prayer. It is a moving prayer. Your body becomes the prayer.

Becoming The Dance

Begin to practice this shamanic way of danced prayer by going into some natural place. You might bring a drum or rattle, or you might pick up something from the ground which makes a rhythmic or rustling sound. A handful of long dry grass can be shaken together. You can tap rhythms on a hollow log with a stick or stone. A pine twig with dried needles still attached makes a good rattle. Two stones or sticks can be clapped together. Flowing water can be splashed. In this way you honor the spirits of the place by joining your dance to theirs.

As your dance shapes itself, as your music finds its pulse, become aware of your own feelings. Your feelings become the dance. You may be moved to ecstatic praise, or you may simply find the means to address a particular request to the spirits. On the other hand, if you are feeling angry or sad, dance out the feeling and at the same time ask for that which will transform the situation to a more positive one. If you are feeling loving, send the love forth on a danced prayer to all life.

As the mystery of the creation fills you, let your prayer become one with that mystery. Dance, make music and sing or chant for as long as you are joined to and caught up in the universal flow. Your moving prayer might be very brief, or the energy might extend it into a longer dance. Your dance can be quite simple. Your chant can be one word of praise or prayer repeated in time with your movement. Or you can really let go and leap about in spontaneous dance and song. Simply let the mystery power enter you. Dance, move, speak and chant spontaneously. Let the medicine power take you where it will.

As always, when you are finished, thank all the spirits who have opened themselves to you and joined you in the dance.

SHAMANIC TRANCE JOURNEY

Shamanic trance journeys are usually among the first things to be mentioned whenever shamanism is discussed or written about. Shamans enter an altered state of consciousness in order to go on spirit journeys to the various spirit worlds. There they seek guidance, wisdom, healing powers and magical powers from the spirit beings of those realms.

The methods and techniques traditional shamans

Earth Ecstasy

use to enter altered states and to journey to the spirit worlds are endlessly described and studied by anthropologists and other social scientists. Furthermore, certain neo-shamanic teachers attempt to duplicate these native or indigenous techniques in their writings and seminars. And all of this can seem a little overwhelming. It doesn't have to be. You don't need to master an entire complex of strange technologies to begin making spirit journeys or entering shamanic trance states. Although you may not realize it, you have been doing very similar things for most of your life.

The human spirit knows how to trance—and needs to. You've already been in an altered trance state many times without realizing it. Watching T.V. or a movie and being deeply absorbed in it is a light trance state. If you daydream and surprise yourself when you notice how much time has passed, you have the capacity to move into a light trance. And that's about all you need to begin exploring spirit journeys.

Then, too, if you are living in a way that respects Earth Mother, there's a pretty good chance you have nature spirit helpers or guardians who will welcome communication with you. And that's one of the main reasons why people undertake spirit trance journeys in the first place—to connect with helpers in the spirit world. Later in this section I will give you some specific guidance to help you journey to the realm of the Nature Spirits and encounter your animal spirit helpers. For now, though, consider these preparations and general directions for undertaking any movement into a naturally altered state of consciousness.

Find a place that's quiet, a place where you don't have to stay alert to what's going on around you. (Don't enter trance states while you're driving, for example, or running a power saw!) Some people find that rhythmic sounds help them enter the trance state. (Shamanic drumming cassettes can be purchased at most metaphysical bookstores.) Others prefer darkness and silence and still others play relaxing, meditative music. Many people find a particular body posture helpful, too. Most people prefer lying down. But you can experiment with all this and discover what's best to help you relax and open yourself to inner journeying.

Many people prefer to go on spirit trance journeys at night, for at night there is less separation between the earth and spirit realms. At this time we have better access to our dreamselves and our magical selves. But we can go on spirit journeys in the daytime as well.

Your spirit is predisposed to trancing, so you don't have to force it. Let the journey travel you rather than you trying to make the journey. And be open to experiencing the journey in any number of ways. You may see it happening, or you may feel it happening to you. It may present itself through one or more of your senses or it may come to you at a level of sensing words can't describe. If at any time you feel uncomfortable, simply return to a state of waking awareness.

Also be aware that you can hinder your journeying by trying to analyze things as they are happening or by trying to make sure you're doing it correctly or by constantly asking yourself, "Have I entered a trance state yet?"

If we think we must always be serious when we enter the spirit realm, we will miss the joy of the experience.

Earth Ecstasy

Too many non-tribal, modern people think they must have a goal-oriented, businesslike mindset on their spirit journeys. That is a good way to miss the joy, the ecstasy and the sheer adventure of such journeys. Serious joy, or sacred play, is very much a part of the shamanic worldview.

Therefore, if you encounter some absolutely hilarious experiences during the spirit journey but are determined to make this "a serious matter," you may very well miss an important connection with some very playful spirits. Spirit beings are often humorous and delightful. Enjoy, and glean their wisdom as you learn in laughter. A sense of play, joy and wonder is not going to get in the way of your journey, but will often enhance your experiences in the spirit world.

Being judgmental is equally frustrating. Try to avoid having a preconceived notion of what a spirit journey should be. Don't decide beforehand that the journey has to be glamourous or that you have to encounter "important" animal spirits. You might miss out on a very deep encounter with a Mouse or a Gopher Spirit. Furthermore, if you dismiss any experience you may have as "just my imagination," you're putting down the very means by which we most readily enter spirit worlds. Our imaginations bring us on spirit journeys in the first place. Our imaginations are the way spirit speaks to us. A spirit journey may not feel different than any other vivid exercise of the imagination; it's just more intentional.

Our spirits, freed at last from the bonds of mundane reality, might wander to realms not thought of before the journey to have different experiences and adventures than those we set out to have. So let your spirit guide you, and visit the wonderful worlds that unfold. Be patient. When you go on spirit journeys often enough you will find that your spirit will move more purposefully.

One of the most important spirit journeys that shamans take is the journey to the Nature Spirit realm to meet with Animal Spirit Guardians and other Nature Spirits from which to get wisdom, guidance, help, healing and power. This realm is also known as the Lower World, for it is deep in the heart of Earth Mother and is reached by spirit travel far below the surface of the earth.

There are many spirit realms to which you may travel. After you've gone to one realm, your spirit will often lead you to others. However, the Lower Realm is a good place to start with because journeying there is fairly easy. After all, this is Earth Mother's realm, and as Her children we are welcome to her mystery realm. Your Nature Spirit Guardians await you in the Lower World and will therefore help you get there.

I will present a guided journey as a way to help you get started. Follow the guidelines above for entering a light trance state. You could have someone read this aloud to you in a slow, serene voice; or read it yourself into a tape recorder and play it back, or simply read it over a few times and remember it. (Three dots ... indicates a long pause in the reading.)

Spirit Journey To The Lower World

Lie down and relax...Begin to breathe deeply, allowing yourself to completely relax...Visualize, feel and sense yourself walking through a beautiful forest...You can hear the birds singing in the trees...You can smell the

58

Earth Ecstasy

freshness of the forest...You can see the dappled sunlight filter through the leaves. As you walk, you are looking for a special tree, a tree that is so large that its branches seem to reach to the sky. A tree whose roots are so big and sturdy that they seem to grow to the center of the earth ... And now, in the distance, you see this tree of life...you approach the tree and realize that there is an opening, a small hollow doorway at the base of the trunk...You enter the tree and see that you can slide or climb down the hollow roots into the realm of the Nature Spirits. You begin to journey down, down...deep down into the heart of Earth Mother.

When you arrive in the realm of the Nature Spirits, look around and familiarize yourself with this world. If you meet any animals, plants or other spirit beings, greet them and speak to them...Listen for their answer in return. Their answer might come in words or in actions. Ask them for advice or help and notice what they say or do in response. Then ask how you might serve them and all of nature... When you are through, thank any beings you saw or interacted with, and return the way you came.

When you journey on your own, you will probably find various ways to enter the Lower World. Although many people enter the Nature Spirit realm through a natural opening in the earth—a cave, a hollow tree trunk, a hot spring or other body of water—the ways to enter are as varied as the people going there. And although many people travel down a tunnel to get there, others find their own unique way.

Shamans also journey to the celestial realms to meet cosmic spirits to obtain help and healing, guidance and power from them, as well. You might try to journey upwards through the hollow branches of the same tree in whose roots you just went to the Lower World. Or you might find your own way there.

Before you embark on a spirit journey, you may decide on a question or problem to which you seek an answer, or you may simply let the spirits you encounter decide what you need to learn or do there. Sometimes you journey for a particular purpose, sometimes merely for a visit. Some teachers tell you to go with a mission or a question every time. I feel that is as opportunistic as going to a friend's house only to borrow something or seek advice. I believe it is often better to go simply because you love to be with your spirit friends and because being together leads to spontaneous sharing, healing, or learning.

Remember, the advice you get from the world of spirits is just that—advice. It is ultimately up to your good judgement whether you will follow it or not.

Many primal societies make spirit journeys, spirit visions and spirit learnings available on the earth plane by enacting these experiences as rituals, ceremonies or stories.

It is a good idea to act out and dramatize your experiences after you return from a spirit journey. Or write them down. Or live them out. Make them manifest here in some way on the earth plane if you can. For only then will their power, healing and wisdom fully affect mundane reality.

While on a spirit journey you may be given a gift from a spirit being—a crystal, a sacred pouch, an amulet, or a symbolic pendant, for example. Receive it with thanks. When you are done with the journey, you might ask the spirit being to keep it for you until you return, or you may bring your gift back in spirit. In any event, be on the lookout for the gift in the mundane world. You may eventually find it or something quite like it on this plane, as well.

Finally, the more you journey, the better you get at it. In time you will easily be able to take many journeys to the Nature Spirit realm or other spirit realms.

VISION QUEST

The animal spirits and the other nature spirits, as we have already seen, have much to teach us. One way we can open ourselves to their teaching in an especially focused and intentional way is the vision quest.

Some version of the vision quest—going off alone to a special or remote place to fast and pray—occurs among all tribal peoples the world over. We, too, can undertake this spiritual endeavor, especially when we seek some basic renewal or reach some turning point in our lives. But we can also undertake smaller vision quests. This might mean, for example, skipping a meal or eating lightly and then finding a quiet corner of a backyard or park to stay silent in for some hours. We can pray for a vision of how best, how wisely, to live our lives.

Whether we are on a short or an extended vision quest, we should simply stay open to everything that occurs. The smallest natural phenomena can be Earth Mother's way of speaking to us on our vision quest. The smallest insect crossing your path might well bring you a message from spirit.

Shamanic Wisdom

Sometimes our answer comes in a vision, or in words we hear within our minds or hearts. More often, the message comes directly from nature Herself, in the form of small changes in the surroundings, in the appearance of insects or birds or animals, or in changes in the weather. For example, perhaps the wind begins to sigh, and you can hear a word or a message in the sound. Perhaps something unusual occurs, like the sound of thunder on a clear day, or a shooting star if you are questing at night. Perhaps an animal or a bird that is not usually in that area makes an appearance. On the other hand, nothing unusual at all might occur, and yet, you may receive your answer from a series of very common natural events. A bee works diligently on the flowers, an ant walks by carrying something, the wind dies down suddenly and all is still, two hawks circle together in the sky as the sun breaks through an overcast day. If you observe these common events carefully enough you will discern an element in them that is unique or that somehow applies to your life. This is how Earth Mother replies to our prayers on the vision quest. That is why we observe everything.

It is best to wait for the vision quest to end, before you begin analyzing your message. If you get analytical and logical during the quest, chances are you will not be able to pay full attention. Sometimes it takes months or years for the full meaning of the message to unravel. The most important and meaningful messages are often the ones that take many years to unfold, as we garner the wisdom and the life experiences necessary to understand them. Therefore, although your vision quest ends, the lifetime work of fully and deeply realizing the message goes on.

Earth Ecstasy

In this way we might often go on little vision quests. From time to time we might also go on more extended, ambitious quests. However we choose to do it, this spiritual exercise involves at least these basic elements:

__ Getting prepared through getting one's self cleaned out. Giving up sugar, caffeine, alcohol and nicotine can be as useful to some people as abstaining from food is to others.

__ Getting quiet. We go off alone to some place in nature where we're unlikely to be interrupted by mundane concerns. This usually requires going to an isolated place for one or more days. We walk about until we find a spot that calls to us. Then we stay at that spot for the entire vision quest.

__ Getting aware. There in nature we watch and listen and sense with all our powers of receptivity. We offer prayers and make requests to the spirits.

The biggest mistake many of us make on a vision quest is constantly seeking a great vision or an unusual natural phenomena, and ignoring the message sent to us by a crow, an ant, a breeze. You may see something as ordinary as a bird taking flight reminding you to aspire to great heights. You may see an event as common as leaves falling telling you to let go of something. Allow yourself to come to understand how even subtle or everyday natural occurrences may be alerting you to change some habit or stay steady in some goal.

After you return to the everyday world, give thanks often for the messages you have received and meditate on them to allow their full significance to blossom forth in your life.

CHAPTER 5
SENDING A VOICE

PRAYER, ASKING, INVOKING

When you walk the shamanic path, you share in the life of a conscious creation. You are aware that all of creation is alive—trees, waters, grasses, insects, fishes, animals, stones and stars. You recognize that all these beings have their own wisdom, a wisdom they make available to us and powers they will share with us—if we but ask. Like many tribal peoples, you will come to regard the animals and plants as your grandparents and the rocks and stones as your great grandparents. These beings have evolved long before the human species and have witnessed human evolution. So they know how much we need to learn from them and be guided by them. The past several hundred years, and especially the past few decades, have shown how destructive humans become when they divorce themselves from nature and try to go it alone. Clearly, it is time to renew our ancient bond with the Nature Spirits and to walk in the protection of their understanding and assistance.

We can renew these connections by praying to the Nature Spirits, invoking their aid and asking for their instruction regularly. And we can also direct our prayers and invocations to the spirits of our ancestors and to our own guardian spirits among the plant, animal and mineral clans. As children of Earth Mother, we can also turn to Her in our need. She gave us our lives. We come from Her body. She responds to us, for we are Her own flesh and blood.

Some traditional peoples call praying "sending a voice." You can do that, too. You can send your voice to the wise and ancient trees, plants, rocks and animals right in your own backyard whenever you need help. And they will hear you. They will respond or will relay your cry to the powers most able to help you.

When we modern people think of praying, we think of getting on our knees and bowing our heads. This is really only one of many ways to pray, and it is the most humbling. Shamanic praying is different from this, for it enlivens us and fills us with power. It inspires us and fills us with life, hope and a belief in our own inner strength. Half the prayer is answered right there during the prayer, for the very process of praying empowers us.

Prayer to the Nature Spirits, to Earth Mother, to the Creator is most effective when it comes from the heart, when we put all our energy and feeling into it. A good, powerful prayer is a matter of will, emotion and belief— W.E.B.: Will, Emotion, Belief, the web that weaves us all together. If you find yourself sad or happy or feeling anything deeply, send a prayer on that feeling. Nature Spirits respond to emotion and the language of the heart better than they respond to just words alone. Emotions send a prayer soaring. If you're feeling longing, sadness or need when you pray, express these emotions as part of your prayer. If you're feeling joyous and happy, prayers of thanks and praise are in order. When these emotion-filled prayers express themselves rhythmically—in heartfelt songs, chants or dances—all the better. The energies of Earth Mother move rhythmically, too. So you might well be moved to dance, clap your hands, make music, chant or sing—simply and spontaneously. For example, you could create a spontaneous prayer and set it to a beat, as you shake your rattle and repeat a simple prayer over and over, i.e., "I ask for health, I ask for wholeness." Or you might experiment with rhyme by making up very simple ones like, "Spirits of the Oak and Pine, let ancient wisdom now be mine." The Nature Spirits love rhyme.

Or you may send your prayer forth with the power of dance. As you are creating rhythm and chanting your prayer, you might also begin moving your body and allowing yourself to feel, in your heart, the need that motivates the prayer. Then your whole body, your whole self, becomes a moving, singing prayer. Put yourself into it completely and let yourself go. Be as loud and as forceful as you feel. Or be as gay and lighthearted as you feel. Or as wild and abandoned as you feel.

On the other hand, suppose you are feeling low energy, depressed or low-key. Then let your prayer reflect your true feelings. Let yourself experience the sadness as you pray for it to change. If you cry, this is good. Let the emotion carry the prayer to all spirit beings of empathy and kindness, who will be touched by your plight. Touch your tears with your hands, and hold the tears up so the powers of the world can see them. Show your tears to the Nature Spirits, for they are more graphic, emotional and visual than they are verbal. Be as heartfelt as you can sincerely be. Then the prayer is truly heard, for it is filled with honesty, with emotions, with life. At other times you might just express your prayer in spontaneous movement without words. In these various ways your energies join the energies of creation in prayer.

So you can see that praying, as we are talking about it here, isn't a matter of particular postures at special times in buildings set aside for that purpose. Rather it is the act of opening ourselves to the enlivening and empowering energies of our relatives in creation. It is our readiness to let our most heartfelt longings overflow into the universal energies, the only place those longings can be satisfied.

Many of us have not prayed in so long that we have no idea how to begin, but that is no problem. Just go out into your yard or to a park, touch any natural being that calls to you and speak from your heart: "Tree Spirits, please give me the strength and the stability I need to meet the challenges I now face." or "Grass Spirits, please fill me with patience towards my children." or "Flower Spirits, please help me attract love into my life, for I am lonely."

When you pray to one tree or one flower you also call upon the spirit of all trees or all flowers. These are the Tree Spirits and the Flower Spirits. Nature Spirits hold in their very being the collective consciousness and wisdom of their species. Therefore, Nature Spirits make excellent teachers, guides and helpers. A Tree Spirit, for instance, represents the experience and understanding of all trees who are living or have ever lived. And when you are finished praying, be sure to give them thanks.

If a nature being does not live in your locale, you can visualize it and then say a simple, heartfelt prayer like, "Lion Spirits, grant me courage and boldness."

When we pray to the Nature Spirits, it is good to make the prayer as explicit and as graphic as possible and also to link our prayer to that particular Nature Spirit in some concrete way. Prayer feathers, prayer leaves and prayer stones can help us do this.

Prayer Feather

Enlist the help of the Bird Spirits by taking a piece of paper and writing or drawing on it what you seek. Make the picture or sentence a simple one. Then tie the paper to a feather with a bit of string. Hold the prayer feather near your heart and pray to the Bird Spirits for that which you need. Visualize the wish going into the feather. Then put your prayer feather outdoors where the birds can see it. You might tie it to a tree branch, for instance. The Bird Spirits will send your prayer to the four corners of the world.

You can also make a prayer leaf and tie it to a tree so that the Tree Spirits can receive your prayer and send your prayer to Earth Mother through its roots and to Sky Father through its branches. You can make a prayer stone and place it on the ground so that the Stone Spirits can relay your prayer to Earth Mother. You can make a prayer shell and then toss it into a natural body of water as you ask any water being to hear your prayer. You can tie your written prayer to any being in nature that is alive and growing as well. So you might make a prayer flower by tying your prayer to a daisy. Or you might make a prayer tree by tying your piece of paper to a tree. Your prayer is much enhanced if it is written on recycled, biodegradable paper.

We can pray to any Nature Spirit for anything. But it is especially powerful to pray to a nature being for a specific thing that they'd have special knowledge of. For instance, you might pray to Otter for more fun and playfulness in your life or to Badger when you need to be assertive or to Eagle when you need to see clearly and with perspective, and so forth. In the next section I present a list of some nature beings and their special qualities, powers and attributes.

Invoking

There are times, too, when you will call upon particular spirits to fill you with their strengthening and empowering energies. This is often referred to as invoking. Invocation is a form of prayer you use to call the powers of various spirit and nature beings into yourself. When we're invoking we're actually inviting a spirit being either to live within us or to stay around us so that we might share in their power.

As you go through your daily life, you can invoke power and healing from these sources. We can invoke any positive energies or deities including Gods, Goddesses, nature beings, angels, ancestors, Earth Mother, Sun Father and so forth.

On a daily basis we can do this simply by visualizing a particular Nature Spirit and calling upon it. For instance, perhaps you need to become more adaptable and clever. You might visualize Fox and say something like, "Fox Spirits, I am calling to you. Live within me and fill me with your cleverness." Some people find it helpful to look at a picture or statue of the Nature Spirit they are invoking. Others hold an object in their hands, one that they associate with the being they invoke. For example, a sea shell might help us invoke any of the beings who live in the ocean. Of course, if the nature being can be found in your vicinity, it is best to go directly to it. Be with it, touch and see that nature being as you invoke its spirit to live within you and empower you.

You can also invoke nature beings by emulating them. For example, if you are invoking the Tree Spirits, then stand as a tree. Wave your arms over your head like leaves; imagine your feet rooted to the earth; and call upon the tree spirits to live in you. Here is a tree invocation I use. You could try it or, better yet, create your own.

Tree Spirit Invocation

> *Tree Spirits, I am calling on you.*
> *Tree Spirits, be here now!*
> *I need your strength and stability.*
> *Tree Spirits, live in me!*

This invocation lends itself to calling all kinds of Nature Spirits by changing it a little. For example, you might change it to call upon Crystal Spirits by saying, "I need your wisdom and clarity. Crystal Spirits, live in me!" or "I need your grace and mystery. Cat Spirits, live in me!"

and so forth. Invocations do not have to rhyme. Another example of invoking might involve a series of processes such as visualizing, deep breathing and emulating the nature being while speaking simply in your own words. Let's say that you are feeling lost, literally or figuratively. Eagle can never be lost, for he flies higher and higher and sees with great clarity over long distances.

Invoking Eagle

Visualize Eagle...Breathe in and breathe Eagle deep within you...Close your eyes and become Eagle... Spread your arms like wings and call like Eagle. Now ask the Eagle Spirits to enter you, to live in your heart, to help you find your way, to see clearly, to gain the long view, so that you may look far. Breathe in deeply again and feel Eagle filling you with clarity and perspective. Thank Eagle when you are done.

You can invoke briefly, even in public places. For instance, you could simply visualize Eagle, breathe him into yourself and ask him quietly to come to you with his powers.

Another example of a brief invocation is this one to the Mountain Spirits:

Mountain Spirit Invocation

"Mountain Spirits, I call upon you to enter my heart and bring me your stability." Now visualize a mountain, and feel yourself standing as a mountain, strong and stable, on the earth..."Mountain Spirits, I give thanks for your friendship and help."

72

Sending A Voice

If you should be feeling especially aimless one day, you might invoke Beaver to fill you with a sense of purpose. You might say, "Beaver Spirits, live in me and fill me with the power to work towards my goal." If you are depressed, you might call in Sun Father, visualizing sunlight filling you as you ask for happiness and optimism. If you are frightened, invite or invoke a courageous animal like Bear, or Lion or Wolf to enter your heart and fill you with courage.

One way some primal peoples invoke or invite the Nature Spirits into themselves is to adorn themselves as the being they're inviting in and then dancing or moving as that being. We can do that,too. Our adornment might not be as elaborate. Our dance might not be formalized—yet we can still honor our natural brothers and sisters and invite them to live in our hearts so as to empower and enliven us. So instead of an entire Bird costume, we might wear a feather and then move and dance as Hawk to invoke Hawk's powers of soaring freedom into ourselves. Or you might want to invoke the independence, grace and mystery of Cat into yourself. You might paint whiskers on your face, cut out pointed cat ears and put them on your head. Then, as a friend beats a drum, or you provide your own rhythm with a rattle, you might move and dance and feel yourself become Cat. As you move, you also can make cat sounds or call out a verbal invocation, e.g., "Cat, I honor you! Cat Spirits, live in me that I may be graceful, mysterious and free!" Or perhaps you seek physical power and strength. You might then dance Horse into yourself. When invoking a Nature Spirit in this manner, really let yourself go and you will feel the nature being you've called upon filling you with its energies and powers. When you are done, sit or lie down and see whether there is a message for you from that being.

To sum it up, you may invoke by visualizing or verbally calling in, or by moving like that being, or by breathing in that being or even by dressing up as that being— anything that helps you identify with the being you wish to invoke, so that you may take on their qualities and powers.

Invoking can be as long and elaborate or as brief and simple a process as you like. It is as important to invoke as you wait in line at the store as it is to do it in more relaxing places or more elaborate ceremonies. We want to get to the point where we can shift our awareness and raise our spirits everywhere.

In any event, the more you know about your relatives in the natural world, the more likely you are to turn to the appropriate one—anytime and anywhere—for that spirit's special help. In any given day, for instance, you might invoke the Lake Spirits to help you be tranquil, the Squirrel Spirits to help you be prudent and wise in saving for a rainy day, the Dolphin Spirits for wisdom and so forth. And no matter which of the ways you use to invoke these spirits (those described above or ones you create for yourself), remember to thank them whether or not they respond to you. For sometimes their response comes, but you don't realize it right away.

Indeed, prayers of thanksgiving are appropriate anytime, not just when our cries have been heard or help has been given us. To offer prayers of thanks is, after all, the most basic way of recognizing the great gift of life itself, of remembering where we come from, of keeping in mind who our allies and relatives are. When we offer prayers of thanks, we open our heart and thus increase our capacity for all kinds of prayer. When we offer a prayer of thanks we acknowledge our dependence upon our sacred Earth Mother and our interdependence with all beings. Thus we make our own wholeness and healing more possible by the very act of prayer.

THE WAY OF THE ANIMAL SPIRITS

Walking the shamanic path means increasing your familiarity with nature. Besides spending more time outdoors, you can also begin studying and reflecting on the ways of nature beings as well. To help you get started, here is a partial list of animals and some of their specific powers and attributes to call upon when praying to them or invoking them. It is a good idea, however, to get to know these animals through communicating with them in the ways presented in this book and to come to know for yourself each animal's powers and gifts.

BADGER: Badger is totally fearless. Call upon Badger for courage, boldness and the ability to hold on to what is yours.

BEAR: Just as all bears retreat to a den when their food becomes scarce, so will Bear teach us to go within—there to meditate and find comfort, wisdom and answers from our deepest selves—when our own lives become difficult.

Shamanic Wisdom

AMERICAN BLACK BEAR: She is a very secretive and intelligent animal. Invoke her ample powers of intelligence when you are studying or pursuing any intellectual endeavor. American Black Bear can teach us to keep the secrets we should and to be comfortable with silence.

GRIZZLY BEAR: A great salmon fisher, Grizzly Bear will help give us the energy we need to pursue our desires, no matter how elusive or slippery they are.

POLAR BEAR: Even though she lives in a very cold and hostile environment, Polar Bear is well adapted to survive and thrive there. Call upon her when life seems cold and people are hostile. Her powerful medicine can keep us warm inside and teach us to glean emotional nourishment from any situation.

BEAVER: Beaver builds canals, lodges and dams. Call upon Beaver when building anything: dreams, a new life, a career.

CHEETAH: As the fastest animal on land, Cheetah's medicine has to do with making progress quickly, accelerating our own growth and expediting any situation.

COYOTE: While most wild predators are diminishing, Coyote thrives and increases because he is so adaptable in every way. Pray to Coyote to help us adjust and thrive in any situation.

DEER: Always alert and aware of danger, Deer teaches us to notice immediately any emotional, spiritual, psychological or physical danger and to leave it in a hurry.

DOG: Pray to Dog Spirits to teach you how to love unconditionally.

EAGLE: Just as Eagle soars high, so does she inspire our spirits to soar. And just as Eagle sees far, so does she foster perspective. Pray to Eagle for transcendence, cosmic awareness, clarity of vision and the will to realize your highest self.

ELEPHANT: Elephants enjoy excellent memories, learning abilities, longevity and loyalty to each other. Call upon Elephant for these attributes.

FOX: Fox's medicine powers include cunning, adaptability, wit, craftiness and cleverness.

HORSE: Horse's sense of vision is very wide. She can see all around her easily. We invoke Horse medicine when we want to get a broad picture and gain perspective.

LEOPARD: Leopard's medicine has to do with speed, timing and camouflage. Call upon her for these powers.

MOUSE: Living close to the earth, Mouse notices every little thing as she forages for food. Invoke Mouse to learn to appreciate the little joys in life.

OTTER: Quickly and efficiently meeting his food demands each day, Otter has much time for fun and play. We can pray to Otter when we want to get a job done quickly but well. We also invoke Otter to open our hearts to joy, laughter and a sense of play.

PRAIRIE DOG: Prairie Dog digs burrow systems that can be as vast as 160 square miles. Their large populations live peaceably in their towns. Call upon Prairie Dog for the wisdom to live happily in an urban environment.

SKUNK: Skunk defends himself very effectively without physically harming others. Call upon skunk to learn creative assertiveness that is effective but not hurtful.

SQUIRREL: Call upon Squirrel if you have a hard time saving for a rainy day or planning ahead. Just as she buries her nuts for the winter, so Squirrel can inspire us, when we pray to her or invoke her, to be prudent with our money and to build our savings.

TIGER: Since Tiger must make many attempts before she succeeds in catching a meal, call upon her for persistence and the spirit to try and try again.

WOLF: Since Wolf mates for life, call upon Wolf for romantic love or to help you find your life mate. Invoke Wolf spirit into you help you increase your loyalty.

THE WAY OF THE TREE SPIRITS

Trees have very ancient and powerful gifts to offer humankind. No matter where you live, in the country or in the city, there will probably be at least one tree in your locale.

All trees foster stability, practicality, serenity, peace and wisdom. Here is a partial list of the medicine powers of various trees. As you walk the shamanic path, it is good, ultimately, to find for yourself what each tree holds as its gift for you as an individual.

FRUIT TREES: All fruit trees hold powerful medicine of abundance, prosperity and fulfillment. While eating a piece of fruit, it is very simple to pray for these gifts. When you are finished, plant the seeds outdoors and visualize your abundance growing like a healthy fruit tree.

ALDER: Harmony, integrity, balance and will-power are Alder's gifts.

APPLE TREE: Besides abundance, Apple Tree's

particular medicine fosters love, romance and passion.

ASH: Compassion, sensitivity, truth and serenity are this tree's medicine gifts.

ASPEN: This tree helps foster unity, intuition and forgiveness.

BIRCH: Moderation, meditation and tolerance are the medicine powers of Birch.

CEDAR: Pray to Cedar for purification, cleansing and renewal.

CHERRY TREE: The Cherry Tree promotes success, achievement and productiveness.

DOGWOOD: Invoke this tree for loyalty, creativity, spiritual attainment and harmony.

EUCALYPTUS: Healing, kindness, nurturing and spiritual love are the medicine powers of Eucalyptus.

FIG TREE: The medicine powers of happiness, energy and hope are associated with Fig Trees.

FIR: Ancient wisdom, deep meditation and purification are the medicine powers of Fir.

MAPLE: Maple offers us healing, positive thinking and luck.

OAK: Stability, steadfastness and protection are the powers of Oak. An acorn is a protection amulet you can carry with you. But be sure to plant it after awhile so that it can fulfill its mighty promise. Then pick up another acorn and carry that one around awhile for protection.

PEAR TREE: Pear Trees foster generosity, optimism, faith and hope.

PINE: Inner growth, tenacity and ancient wisdom are the gifts of Pine. Find the oldest pine or fir tree in your area and pray to it for the wisdom and knowledge of the ancient ways.

REDWOOD TREE: Invoke Redwood Tree Spirits for longevity, strength, memory and maturity.

SEQUOIA: Relaxation, contentment and peace are Sequoia's special properties.

WALNUT TREE: Pray to this tree for self-reliance, confidence and energy.

WILLOW: Mystic visions, knowing the future, mental telepathy and all psychic powers are the medicine of this lovely tree.

Two trees who grow close to each other and intertwine understand love, friendship and romance. Pray to such trees for these gifts.

Large city trees that grow between the sidewalk and the street are good luck because they were spared while the trees all around them were cut down. Pray to such trees for good luck. Saplings and pine cones grant us the gift of new beginnings.

THE WAY OF THE MINERAL SPIRITS

You can carry minerals around with you in a pouch, in a pocket, on a pendant or embedded in a ring to infuse you with their medicine powers.

AGATE: Love, prosperity, luck, courage, protection, balance and an appreciation of nature are Agate's medicine powers.

AMBER: Romantic love, purification, wisdom, energy, patience and past life recall are gifts of Amber.

AMETHYST: This lovely stone bestows spiritual awareness, meditation, balance, psychic abilities, inner peace, understanding of death and rebirth.

CRYSTALS (clear quartz): Wisdom, clarity of thought, general healing, memory, communication, transformation, awakening, cleansing, pureness of heart, higher consciousness, positive thoughts, meditation, harmony and love—all are Crystal's gifts. Crystals also amplify prayers, wishes and visualizations.

CRYSTAL CLUSTERS (clear quartz): They provide us with protection, harmony and friendship because they break up negative energy in the environment.

DOUBLE-TERMINATED CRYSTALS: These special crystals foster dream recall, psychic ability, and easier access to the spirit world.

DIAMOND: This stone bonds relationships and fosters longevity, innocence, abundance, courage, purity, hope and love. Diamonds also help us get to the essence of things.

FLUORITE: Intellect, consciousness, aura cleansing, truth, and protection are promoted by Fluorite.

GOLD: Virtue, happiness, honor, wealth, generosity, positive thoughts, opportunity, good humor and courage are Gold's gifts.

JADE: For increased practicality, wisdom, tranquility, balance, moderation and stability, pray to Jade.

MOONSTONE: Moonstone promotes humanitarian love, safe travel on water, hope, and new beginnings; helps us get in touch with our feelings.

OBSIDIAN: Inner growth, positive change, fulfillment, introspection, stability, and psychic development are the medicine powers of Obsidian.

SILVER: Grounding, mystic visions, nurturing, hope and meditation are all associated with Silver.

TIGER'S EYE: Empowerment, integrity, clear thinking, willpower and courage are the gifts of Tiger's Eye.

TURQUOISE: Empathy, love, general healing and emotional sensitivity are all nurtured by Turquoise.

CHAPTER 6

ANIMAL SPIRITS, LIVE IN ME!

ANIMAL SPIRIT GUARDIANS

One of the most important ways those on a shamanic path acquire power, protection, help, healing and guidance is through relationship with their animal spirit guardians. And each of us is born with a particular animal helper or guardian whose wisdom, strength and friendship teaches and guards us as we go through life.

We humans are often quite arrogant in our views of animals, regarding them as less conscious, less intelligent than ourselves. Once we make contact with our animal spirit guardian, we can no longer think of animals as "dumb." We see all of nature in a new way; we come to appreciate and revere the great wisdom and love of all the beings in nature.

Animal spirit guardians, once living animals, now live on the spirit plane, choosing to keep the animal form they once had on earth. They were very successful animals when they lived on the earth plane. They derived great joy from their lives and are still dedicated to experiencing animal being. For example, the Medicine Wolf of its tribe, the strongest, brightest wolf, was the leader of its kind when it was alive. Such a successful wolf intends to keep its wolf form and knowledge for awhile in the spirit world and come to the earth plane to help here as well. It chooses to live with you and in you because it wants to experience corporeal earth plane existence again.

Your animal ally, therefore, is really more than an animal now. It is also a spirit, and so it has powers well beyond those of the incarnate animal it once was. First, it has access to all the knowledge and wisdom of its animal kind. So your animal helper has all the powers associated with its physical life as an animal and all the powers that all the members of its species have developed through countless generations. And so it is that a Raccoon animal guardian, for example, brings all the survival instincts and qualities of living raccoons to the task of helping, healing and protecting you. But it also taps into the wisdom and strength of all the raccoon souls that have ever lived on the physical plane. Another example: if your animal ally is Bear, it is not just a bear: but an embodiment of all the strength, courage and wisdom of every bear that ever lived. It is a singular bear, and it is simultaneously all bears. In addition, an animal spirit may also be able to speak in a way humans can understand; for, being of the spirit, it is now fully connected to its soul. Since all souls are one, it now has access to all the collective soul wisdom and knowledge of the universe.

And yet this spirit is still not ready to give up its

Animal Spirits, Live In Me!

animal form. It still longs to feel, from time to time, the wind rippling through its fur, its powerful body running through the grass, the taste of food, the feel of sunlight—all the pleasures and beauties of the earth plane.

Your animal spirit guardian chose you at birth and lived within you during your childhood, keeping you safe while your body and soul matured. When you ran, played and went out into nature, it went with you—running, moving, delighting in life. In return for keeping you protected and strong, it got to live within you and feel alive. Our animal spirit guardians would like to continue to live within us for a mutually beneficial friendship.

Unfortunately, most of us in the mainstream culture lose contact with our animal spirit guardians long before we become adults. If we were ever aware of their presence, we tend to forget them—never acknowledging or honoring them. And so their interaction with us becomes infrequent, their presence rarely felt and never recognized. They do keep a tenuous contact and will sometimes help us in an emergency, even though we don't realize it or notice them. They keep this contact with us because they would like to renew the relationship. That is why retrieving an animal spirit guardian is surprisingly easy for many people. My experience teaching this process has shown me that sincere effort on our part is rewarded sooner or later.

The process of renewing this relationship is sometimes called "retrieving your animal spirit guardian," and many books and teachers offer specific recipes and lock-step instructions for doing this. In my experience, however, it is the animal spirits who want to retrieve us because they want to live within us to experience life again, to teach us their wisdom and show us how to live in harmony with all the natural and wild beings. Animal spirit beings are very aware that humans now need to learn quickly about stewarding Earth Mother. Therefore, if your purpose in making contact is to empower yourself to be an earth healer and if your intentions are positive and for the good, your animal spirits will facilitate contact. The method you use to begin renewing your relationship with your animal helper, therefore, is less important than your willingness to open yourself to the overtures your helper is always making to you.

Do not let preconceived wishes for a "romantic" animal spirit guardian get in the way of recognizing your animal helper. Each species has its own abilities and insights, and so Mouse and Wolverine are just as important in the cosmic scheme as Eagle and Wolf. Your animal spirit guardian may very well be Rabbit or Sage Grouse, or some other animal considered less than glamorous by our mainstream culture. Remember, the animals choose you—not you them. They know which of their species is most appropriate to you and your needs.

It is best to begin being retrieved by the animal spirit guardian or guardians who chose us at birth because it is easier to renew contact with our original power animals than it is to attract new ones. Once we have a good relationship with our original spirit animals, we can then begin inviting additional animal spirits to live with us.

For example, over the last fifteen years I have been given Bear, Horse, Dolphin, Meercat and Cat as animal allies. The first two had chosen me at birth. Horse and Bear came to live within me almost immediately after I began the process of retrieval that I will present to you in this section.

Animal Spirits, Live In Me!

Dolphin got to know me well when I lived on an island off the coast of Florida, swam with Dolphins, communicated with them and subsequently gave time, money and energy towards helping them survive. Dolphin became my ally after some six months of my attempts to connect with them. Meercat, a member of the Mongoose clan, came as a complete surprise. I didn't even know of Meercat's existence until I saw a television show about them on the cable nature channel. I was extremely moved by them. That very night Meercat came to me in my sleep, teaching me many things, and has been with me ever since. I courted Cat for many years, longing for the animal I've known best and loved so much in this life to honor me with a spirit friend. I have served Cat since childhood, bringing home strays, placing ads in papers and finding them homes. I was born loving, serving and being totally enchanted by them. Cat took many years of journeying, calling, invoking and so forth. Cat proved to me that, just as on the earth plane, Cat Spirits won't come when you call them but come in their own good time. I am glad to say that I have recently been chosen by a Cat Spirit.

There are many methods for renewing contact with our animal powers. Do not feel bound by the suggestions presented here. Many people renew contact in their own creative and unique ways. Remember, there are no valid shamanic recipes that work well for everyone. There are no "experts" in this area other than the animal spirits themselves.

Your animal helper may manifest itself by its frequent physical presence in your life or through a deep attraction you feel when you read or see films about particular animals. You can also discover your animal helper by making an inner spirit journey to what some call the Lower World or the realm of the Nature Spirits, deep in the heart of Earth Mother. There are many ways to make an inner spirit journey to befriend and join with your animal helper. Some people find this trance journey facilitated by rhythmic drumming or rattle sounds. Others prefer soothing music or silence. (You can buy shamanic drumming cassettes or meditation music at most metaphysical bookstores.) I find that the sounds of nature are the most helpful for putting me in the shamanic trance state to journey to the spirit world. Therefore, if you have a totally private, safe place in nature to go on spirit journeys, you might try that. Some use guided journeys like the one below (reading the directions on tape to be played back or having a friend read them), while others internalize the directions by reading them and journey in silence—or use no guiding directions at all. You can experiment with different methods until you find the one or ones that work for you.

The purpose of the following guided spirit journey is twofold: first, simply to learn how to go to the Lower World and, once there, to familiarize yourself with it by exploring it; second, to meet one of your animal spirit guardians. On the first journey you may achieve one or both of these goals.

If you do meet an animal spirit there, ask it if it is your animal guardian. Then ask how you can become closer to him/her. You will hear the answer in your heart, in your mind or in a way you cannot explain. Often, at first, our animals speak to us symbolically by doing something

Animal Spirits, Live In Me!

we can interpret later, after the journey.

If a friend is reading this journey to you, it should be read in a slow, calm voice. Dotted lines (...) mean a substantial pause.

Spirit Journey: Meeting Your Animal Spirit Guardians

Put a shamanic drumming cassette on, have a friend drum, play some taped meditation music or just have silence. Lie down on your back and get comfortable. Many people find darkness or low light helpful. Begin to breathe deeply. With each breath out, let yourself completely relax...

Now let yourself visualize, think or feel, as deeply as you can, that you are walking in a natural place...It is beautiful, quiet and serene. It may be a place you have actually been to, or it may be a place you have never seen before. As you walk, you are looking for a natural entrance to the Nature Spirit Realm. But do not look too hard because your spirit knows how to find it. Enjoy the search, for you are now walking in a beautiful, natural place...This entrance to the Lower World, deep in the earth, may be a cave on a natural body of water such as a spring, a pond or the ocean. It may be a hollow in a tree, a crevice in a rock or any other natural opening...

When you find your entrance, take a good look at it, get comfortable with it, take a peek inside. You may see a tunnel. It may be a tight and cozy tunnel that you can slide down or a wide opening that you can fly down; or it may be a unique way down—not a tunnel at all. Go into the entrance. You may walk, slide, fly, float, swim or climb downward; or go down in your own individual way...Let

89

yourself go down, down, down, to the home of the Nature Spirits, deep within the earth...

When you get there, look around, walk around and explore...You may see an animal of some kind, flying, walking or just being near you... And when you do, ask this animal if it is your spirit guardian. Communicate with it, get to know it... If it is your power animal, ask it if it would like to join you and live within you. If it says yes, breathe it into your body. If it says no, tell it that you understand and that you would like to come here often to get to know it better. Thank it for meeting you here.

Now it is time to return. (If someone is reading this aloud to the journeyer, he may begin a rhythmic drum beat now.) Say farewell for now to any beings you met. If you want to meet them here again, let them know this. Give thanks to them and to this sacred place. If you did not yet meet an animal spirit, say farewell to the place, for this is a sacred place. Bid farewell and give thanks to the trees, rocks and other spirit beings here. Tell all the beings here that you want to return and will visit again soon. Give thanks to this sacred place. And now return the way you came.

(The person reading this aloud might beat the drum louder and more rapidly for the return journey.)

If you achieved any part of this journey the first time, you did well. Some people take longer than others to meet their animal allies. If all you accomplished this time was to find your entrance, that is good. Keep going on this journey or strike out on a journey of your own, for I have never known anyone with good intentions who has not found their animal allies sooner or later.

There are other ways to meet, communicate with and befriend our animal spirit guardians. You can show respect for all the animal species by working to preserve their habitats, by efforts on behalf of threatened species, by learning all you can about the lives and ways of animals you're attracted to, and by letting animals' energies manifest themselves in you.

Just as primal peoples do, you also can invite these energies to express themselves through you by spending time in natural places, doing some of the things animals do there — moving quietly, singing or barking or howling, watching, stalking or hiding. You can set aside special times to dress yourself to resemble an animal you wish to honor or simply paint or decorate yourself in ways that honor all animals and animal spirits. Or you can dance in your animal spirit helper.

We can invoke our animal powers into ourselves by adorning ourselves as an animal and dancing them in. We costume ourselves as an animal to show this animal clan that we respect and honor it by emulating it. If you do not yet know who your animal spirit is, you might adorn yourself in a general way with a feather in your hair or whiskers painted on your face, for example, to call in animal spirit energy in general. If you know who your animal ally is, dress as that animal. Your costume could be very simple, just one symbolic thing, or it could be quite elaborate.

Shamanic Wisdom

Dancing In Your Animal Spirit Guardian

Begin by creating a sacred circle large enough to move around in. Stand inside the circle and pray to your animal spirit guardian to come to you, dance with you, live in you. Then begin to move spontaneously while you shake a rattle, beat on a drum, have a friend create rhythm or play a drumming cassette. As you move, you might also chant, pray, sing or speak, with all your intentions and focus on calling in your animal spirit guardian to dance with you. While you are doing this, a feeling, a visual image, a sound or just an idea of an animal may come to you. Start to move like that animal and make the sounds that it makes. For example, if the image of Cat comes to you, move and vocalize like a cat. Sometimes many animals come. And as they come, you move and sound like them.

When your animal spirit guardian comes, however, its spirit will fill you and will energize your movements. It will feel as though you are that animal, that you know that animal, and your movements will become more than you simply moving your body. Your body and spirit will be enlivened and filled with that animal's power. When this happens, let yourself move into the spirit of that animal and it into you. Move and vocalize in ways that resemble those of your animal helper. Really let yourself go and express your spirit animal fully. (Put down your rattle or drum if it gets in the way of full expression.)

While dancing your animal ally, you might find yourself chanting, speaking, singing or vocalizing some-times as the animal, sometimes as yourself. Continue danc-ing, moving and exchanging energies with your animal

Animal Spirits, Live In Me!

helper until the movement of energies peaks. Then sit or lie down in stillness and allow any messages from your animal helper to form themselves in your mind or heart. See if you can create a dialogue between yourselves. As always, when you have finished, thank your helper and all the other animal spirits who may have presented themselves.

If you are inhibited at first, keep at it. Dance in your animal spirits alone at first, if you are shy. You will eventually give in to the ecstasy and abandonment that is awaiting you and your animal ally. Pray to the animal spirits to help, for they are not self-conscious, and they do not block their own joy of movement. When you are more comfortable, you might dance in your power animal with others present. The spirit animals can interact with each other in such groups, and this makes it an even more lively experience. Dancing in animal powers enlivens, refreshes and empowers us. Once we have retrieved our animal allies, we should dance them in often. This not only vitalizes us, it also strengthens the bond of friendship between ourselves and our spirit animals. Finally, it allows our animals to dance, move and express themselves on the earth plane in a body again. They enjoy this immensely.

Both the spirit journey and dancing in your animals are used initially to allow yourself to be retrieved by your animal allies and are then also used to continue contact with them. There are other ways to continue or foster contact as well. Quartz crystals act as a communication bridge between species. That is why shamans often use a crystal rattle to call in and to dance in their animal spirits. This rattle could simply be a non-breakable container with tiny crystals inside, or it could be a more traditional rattle with small crystals hanging from it.

Dreams offer still another powerfully effective way to meet and communicate with animal spirits.

Meeting Animal Spirits In Dreamtime

Hold a quartz crystal to your heart as you lie down to sleep, and ask the Crystal Spirits to open you to contact with your animal helpers. Then, placing the crystal under your pillow, pray for a visit from your helpers as you fall asleep. Upon awakening, hold the crystal and ask to remember what happened in the dreamtime. Now gaze into the crystal by holding it up at eye level and turning it this way and that. Often you will get a feeling or a visualization of your animal spirit guardian within the crystal.

As you can see, there are many ways to recognize and befriend your animal spirit helpers. Perhaps the methods presented here will stimulate your imagination and creativity in developing still others. But no matter how you renew this relationship, you must still work to keep it strong and flourishing. In addition to the many ways to honor and communicate with the animal spirits I've already described in this section, I would also recommend these practices to be done frequently:

— Communicate with your animal spirit helpers often, even it it's just a brief thought or silent prayer.

— Like the animals, spend as much time as you can in wild and natural places, enjoying these sacred places and caring for them.

— Keep your body healthy and vital so that the

Animal Spirits, Live In Me!

animal spirits will feel welcome and happy whenever you invoke them into yourself.

—Do all you can for animals still incarnate on earth in pragmatic ways. Save them and their habitat from destruction.

CHAPTER 7
MYSTERY POWER

MEDICINE POWER

Medicine power is really a connectedness with all the powers of the universe. What some call medicine power, others call positive magic. I like the term mystery power, however, because it more accurately and directly names the source of such power: our intimate relationship with all the energies of the universe. I will refer to the acquiring, raising and projecting of energy to affect the earth plane as either medicine power or mystery power.

People are given medicine powers from the great sacred mystery that created everything—from the spirit realm, from Earth Mother, from the Creator. But although the medicine power is granted us by Earth Mother and the Creator, often it is brought to us by the Spirit— sometimes in dreams, sometimes in visions, sometimes by the animals and plants and minerals of this plane and of the spirit plane. There are so many ways we can be given medicine power:

we may be granted the gift to heal, or to see true visions, to see the future, to control weather, or to make sacred charms and so forth.

The essential element in acquiring, keeping and directing medicine power is connectedness. All of our efforts on behalf of Earth Mother and all living beings keep us connected with the sources of our mystery power because they keep us connected with the Mystery. The rituals and ceremonies we enact also help us to feel and to realize our connection with the entire universe. As our rituals actions link us with the forces of nature and the great collective subconscious mind of all beings who live and who have ever lived in the universe, we can then project our thoughts, wishes, needs, desires, hopes, prayers and gifts of healing into the universe and affect mundane reality here on earth as well.

Besides being granted a gift of a specific kind of medicine power, we can also raise a more general medicine power to help us carry forth a prayer, a wish or a desire. Every natural thing on earth has its medicine power. We can raise medicine power when we attune ourselves to and ally ourselves with all the beings of nature.

We can direct these forces because we are also a force of nature. We are part of the whole, and the whole is also embodied in each of us. The earth is our Mother and we are the earth, literally and figuratively. The sun is our Father, and we are the sun. We are a part of the universe, and we are the universe.

Although medicine power comes to us in many ways, from many sources, we cannot fully use and direct that power for the good if we are not grounded in a solid relationship with our sacred Earth Mother. Remember, the shamanic path is always rooted deeply, deeply in our connectedness to earth power.

When we raise medicine power in conjunction with the forces of nature, we can best do so by letting our emotions flow and mingle with the nature forces. Emotion is what the Nature Spirits understand best. Emotions within ourselves is like weather on earth. Storms and clouds and rain and sunshine and warmth and coldness and wind and breeze and hurricanes are Earth Mother's emotions—Her many moods, Her various expressions of feelings. Anger and tears and happiness and warmth and coldness and laughter and yelling and high spirits and love are our weather.

And we have seasons just as Earth Mother does. Sometimes it is winter inside us and we feel cool and aloof and withdrawn and sober and inner. And sometimes it is summer inside us and we shine and laugh and express warmth and passion. We play and grow and join with others. To repress our weather, our seasons, takes away our power and turns our emotions bitter and cold. When we express the full range of human emotions, then we don't repress them and turn them into hate and rage. When we combine our emotions with our will and our belief in medicine power then we can raise and direct very powerful magic or medicine power.

Raising Earth Power

Be with nature in all Her many moods and feel Earth Mother's power. Go out and stand in the wind, or the cold or the snow or just before a storm. Raise your arms up

Shamanic Wisdom

and feel Her power enter you. Each day should present itself with many such times. The morning mist, the heat of midday, the afternoon stillness, the evening breeeze, the night chill, the rain, the interplay of bird and insect and grasses—each has its power, each invokes a feeling in us. The feeling it invokes is the power. You can do this in your backyard many times during the day or night, even if it is only for a moment.

This is an excellent way to begin being with Earth Mother more often, and invoking Her power into you.

When you raise medicine power indoors you can remember the feeling you had at these peak moments and reempower yourself by letting that feeling well up in you again.

To raise medicine power means to tap powerful spirit forces and then direct that energy to affect the mundane plane. In order to do this, we first must suspend our cultural ideas of what can and can't be—of what is and isn't possible. Anything can be. Everything is possible. When we raise the mystery power and direct it with our will, through our emotions, we must believe a hundred percent that it is real. That is Mystery Power, Medicine Power, Positive Magic. Will, Emotion and Belief: W. E. B. The WEB that weaves us all together. The Web that connects all. We can tug on that web, and we can add a strand to it, too. And we can also watch in awe, as the world web glitters in the morning sun and dew. And we can dance up and down on the web and make it jiggle. Will, Emotion, Belief: WEB. That's how we join in the dance of Mystery and Power. We get up on that big world web like a tiny spider

100

and we do our thing.

Some modern religious and cultural hierarchical authorities try to rob us of our will, and try to have us repress our emotions and limit our beliefs of what is possibe on this plane. Their goal? Simply that we submit to their authority, build them guilded castles and buy them fancy robes. They rob us of our power. But you can take back your power, you can get back on the web. It is for all of us to dance on, not just those who call themselves religious leaders. There should be zillions of little spiders spinning and creating and tugging away on the web. Each and every one of us born of Earth Mother was born with the ability to make silken thread to spin with. Each of us is an important part of the Mystery. Each of us is magic.

Since we are all relatives with all earth's living beings, we can most easily access the medicine powers of the nature forces. While we can also raise medicine power of the stars and the celestial realms, we who are now incarnate on earth can most easily resonate with the powers of the earth.

And calling upon the forces of nature for assistance is one of the primary ways to raise medicine power. There are as many ways to raise medicine power as there are forces in nature. For example, you might pray during a storm, sending your prayer out on the power of the wind and the force of the thunder. Or while at the beach, you might draw a wish in the sand, and then ask Grandmother Ocean to send forth the prayer on the mystery power of the waves, as high tide carries your prayer forth. On a sparkling clear night you might send forth your prayer on medicine power of the clarity and purity of that evening. In the soft mist of morning you may send a prayer from the heart, and visualize the prayer wrapped in gentle dew falling softly to the earth.

As you can see, the ways you can send forth medicine power in conjunction with nature are as unlimited as your imagination and creativity.

Raising Medicine Power with Thunder-beings

There is great medicine power just before a storm. Go outside and stand with arms upraised in the wind and feel yourself become one with the storm beings. Then begin to beat on your drum or other rhythm instrument. Let the power of the storm's building energy build in your heart. Become the storm, as you move, drum, dance chant or speak out loud, addressing yourself to the Storm Spirits. "Spirits of wind, or rain, of thunder, fill me with your power." When you feel the storm power peak within you, then send a prayer, a visualization, a wish or a desire out on the power of the storm. You might do this by chanting the prayer over and over as you beat your drum loudly, for example. As every gust of wind blows upon you, you might visualize the prayer being blown from your heart to the four corners of the universe. As your heart pounds with the power and the wildness of the storm beings, feel your heart join with the Thunder-beings and envision each heartbeat as a prayer going forth on the power of the storm. You might also pick up a fallen leaf, hold it to your heart and visualize your prayer going into the leaf, then let the leaf go on a gust of wind as you call out your heart's desire into the wind. (It goes without saying that you should do all this just before the storm actually hits, and before the winds become

Mystery Power

dangerously strong.)

When we are given medicine power in any way, then something is required of us, too. We must give back, give thanks in some way.

If we are to live in harmony and in relationship with the spirit forces who give us visions and other medicine powers then we must enact that power on the earth for the good of all life. For what we get from spirit is not just for us alone. If you receive the medicine power to heal, then it is so you can give healing to others. Note the word "give" here, not sell. For example, too many Americans receive the gift of healing from spirit and then turn around and become so called "healers" who charge money for healing. At any rate, it is believed by many primal peoples that if spirit gives you a power, that power cannot be activated until it is ennacted on the earth plane in a giving manner. To sum up, raising medicine power is the ability, through friendship and connectedness with the beings of nature, to harness the forces of nature. The key here, as in all things we consider when we follow the shamanic path, is relationship. All our brothers and sisters in the universe, from the stones to the stars, have their own particular power. The mystery power of whirlwinds and rainstorms, of growth and creativity, of moon and sun and sea—all the forces of nature—are at our call if we are in alliance with nature. Life is at our call if the medicine power we seek to raise is for the benefit of life. But if we do not interact with them, they cannot share their power with us—nor we with them.

As you can see, to develop this ability to work with the forces of nature, to gain medicine power and then raise and direct and shape it so as to affect reality, we must learn as much as we can about nature and attune ourselves to Her. It may take you awhile to discover which beings or forces you are most closely connected to, which are most likely to become your strong friends and allies. In fact, much of this book is devoted to helping you make those discoveries and to open yourself to particular offers to share powers that other beings might make to you. Then, too, once you begin to learn more about the particular sources of your power, you must learn to work with those sources. There are, however, some general principles that seem to appy to this process, some habits of mind and action that native peoples have worked out over many generations.

First, seek harmony with all the forces your encounter. Look for the ways you and they can exist together for the greatest good of all.

Next, learn as much as you can about any and all the beings with whom you feel a special or intimate connection. Discover their preferences and special abilities. Go out of your way to let them get to know you, too.

When you call upon the powers you may have been given or the powers that express themselves through natural forces, always do so with respect and with the will to do good. Whatever we send out will return to us, magnified many times.

Finally, power unused is power lost. When nature or spirit beings share power with you, they do so in order that all living beings may benefit. So with the medicine power comes the obligation to work actively for the welfare of Earth Mother and all living beings. If you are given powers, you are empowered to serve life.

THE SEVEN DIRECTIONS

The shamanic path asks that we orient ourselves to our earthly existence and our cosmic existence at the same time. The seven directions (i.e., East, West, North, South, Above, Below and Center) help us to do this. They are important powers to understand and interact with because they embody all that is life on earth and all that exists in the cosmos. They represent every aspect of human existence as well.

The significance of each of these directions will become clearer to you as you observe and meditate on each one. So what I (or any other writer) have to say about them should be used only as a starting point for your own explorations. For instance, the four cardinal directions are commonly associated with the four elements. However, each tribe and group has its own associations. Right now, before you read any further about the most common associations those of us following a neo-shamanic path currently attribute to the four directions, it would be a good idea for you to discover what the four cardinal directions mean to you. If you merely try to memorize other people's correspondences, you lessen the chance for your own spontaneous relationship with the four directions. I suggest you go outside and do this exercise before you read further.

Exercise: Appreciating The Four Directions

Go outdoors, turn to the east, raise your arms towards the east and tell the Spirits of the East what you appreciate and notice about them, what they mean to you. What you say could be as simple as , "I am glad that the sun rises here every day." Now ask the Spirits of the East to speak to you. Close your eyes and see what feelings, images or thoughts come to you. Do the same for each of the other directions.

Whatever you read about the directions or any other powers of nature is far less important than your own wisdom, insight and relationship built on your personal experiences with them. That is why I stress so strongly that you keep your own experiences in mind as you consider these common, current associations of the four directions:

East is associated with the element Air and the season of spring. East is the place of dawn, where the sun rises each day. New beginnings, renewed hope, innocence, renewal, awakening, enlightenment, and illumination are the gifts and powers of the Spirits of the East. The element Air brings the gifts of intellect, clarity of communication, memory, freedom, independence, quick perception and understanding. The Eagle and other birds are the animals associated with East.

South corresponds to the element Fire in the season of summer. South is the place of midday, aglow with the light of Sun Father. Energy, warmth, brightness, heat, generosity, benevolence, intensity, truth, inspiration, optimism and the ability to bring light to any situation are the gifts and powers of the Spirits of the South. The element Fire brings the gifts of sensuality and sexuality, creativity, romantic love, passion, originality, courage, digestion, assimilation, will, self-confidence, individuality and enthusiasm. Lion and Coyote are the animals associated with South.

West corresponds to the element Water. It is the place of sunsets and the harvest season of autumn. Completion, endings, satisfaction, fulfillment, realization, peace and serenity are the gifts and powers of the Spirits of the West. The element Water brings the gifts of purification, cleansing, consecration, forgiveness, sensitivity, emotional balance, tolerance, compassion, gentle power, devotion, intimacy, imagination, oceanic insight and the open-hearted acceptance of our feelings. Dolphin and other sea beings are the animals associated with West.

North corresponds to the element Earth. North is associated with the season of winter and the time of midnight. As the place where the sun never passes, North is considered a place of great mystery. Secrecy, enchantment, appreciation of mystery, attentive listening (to others and ourselves) and the ability to keep our own counsel are the wisdom, teachings, gifts and powers of the Spirits of the North. The element Earth brings the gifts of stability, vitality, practicality, groundedness, ability to work hard, patience and appreciation of our bodies. Buffalo, Polar Bear and other polar animals are associated with North.

Above is associated with Sky Father, Sun Father and any deities that dwell in the heavens, as well as the powers of the stars, the moon and the vastness of space. It

Shamanic Wisdom

is a place where the planetary and celestial powers hold primacy. This is the place of transcendence, cosmic awareness, unlimited consciousness and universal love.

Below is associated with Earth Mother, the Sustainer of all life, with all the beings who dwell here and with all the spirit powers of this planet. Her many gifts and powers are obvious to us all and become more so as we spend more time following the shamanic path.

At the **Center** we ourselves stand. This is the place where all the powers have come together to manifest themselves in the uniqueness that is each of us. It is the balanced convergence of all the aspects of creation in one incarnate being. It's the place where we seek to live in harmony with all those powers.

Some people make it a practice to greet each of the seven directions when they first awaken each morning, using spoken or silent prayers, facing or gesturing in the appropriate direction for each. (Other people, however, work only with the four cardinal directions on a regular basis.)

Greeting The Seven Directions

Upon arising in the morning, turn to each of the directions with a gesture of greeting or honor. You may or may not say something. For example, in silent greeting each morning you might face, in this order, East, South, West, North, Up and Down. Reach your arms out to them in greeting and let a feeling of respect and friendship and appreciation enter your heart as you do this. Then put your

Mystery Power

hands on your solar plexus in silent greeting to the Center.

Some people concentrate on one particular direction for a period of time if they seek the gifts and insights which reside in that direction. For example, those who want to attract romantic love into their lives might greet, honor, pray to and invoke the Spirits of the South and the element Fire in various ways as they go through the day. Or those seeking a sense of closure to a relationship or to a phase of their lives would turn to the Spirits of the West for help. If a person wants to become more self-disciplined and work-oriented, she might focus on the Spirits of the North and the element Earth. I did this myself when I was younger and not at all disciplined about my writing. I called on the element Earth and its corresponding direction many times a day for several months. I asked the Spirits of North to make me more dependable and work-oriented. So, if there is something you need to invoke into yourself, you can pray to that element or direction, to that power, by facing the direction every day and invoking that into yourself.

Let's say you need to be more patient. That is a power of the element Earth, most commonly associated with the Spirits of the North. You might face North every day, lift your voice in prayer and pray to North for patience. Make it a heartfelt prayer. Remember when others were patient with you as you face North; give thanks for that; visualize yourself being patient with others and with yourself. Tell the spirits how you have been working on being more patient. Give progress reports each day and give thanks to the spirits for your progress. Ask the Spirits of the North for the gift of patience each day until you are given that gift.

Perhaps you need to open your heart. Maybe something has made you bitter and cold. Face West and invoke the Water Spirits on a regular basis. Say something like this, "Powers of the West, Spirits of Water, wash away the bitterness in my soul. Bathe my heart with new innocence and teach me to trust again."

If you seek wisdom, face North and say something like, "Powers of North, Spirits of Air, fill my mind with ancient wisdom and the knowledge of the ancient ways."

As you meditate upon and come to understand more deeply the powers of the directions and elements, you will know which qualities and energies to ask for from each direction and element.

Basically, you want to be able to communicate with the directions and elements and build a relationship with them. There is no proper or fixed way to communicate with the seven great powers of the world. Some people speak aloud to the spirits and animal guardians of each direction. Others turn their attention mentally in that direction and pray silently. However you choose to communicate, remember always to offer thanks respectfully as well as making requests. And always see your prayer as answered, even as you make it.

Because many people cannot just start out communicating spontaneously, I will suggest some things for you to say. Use them to get started if you can't think of what to say right now. Eventually you will.

Mystery Power

Communicating With The Seven Directions

Many people make a gesture of greeting or honor as they speak to the directions. Both arms raised towards the direction is common.

Face East and say, "Spirits of East, Grandmother Eagle, keeper of the dawn, hope of the new day, I give thanks for the sunrise, and I ask you to bathe me in illumination."

Face South, raise your arms towards that direction and say, "Spirits of the South, Coyote, keeper of the flame of creation, I give thanks for heat and passion and ask you to make my will strong."

Face West, raise your arms towards that direction and say, "Spirits of the West, Grandmother Dolphin, daughter of the sunset, keeper of the waters, I give thanks for cleansing rains and ask you to open my heart."

Face North, raise your hands to that direction and say, "Spirits of the North, Grandfather Buffalo, keeper of the Mystery, I give thanks for healing silence and ask that I may grow in patience."

Face Above, raise your arms towards the heavens and say, "Sun Father, radiant Protector of the earth, I give thanks for the love You shower on all life, and I ask that You fill my heart with warm generosity."

Face Down, reach out your arms towards Earth and say, "Earth Mother, sacred Life-Giver, I give thanks for Your bounty and ask for abundance."

Then hold your own belly or solar plexus and say, "I am the Center, and I give thanks for this life, right here, right now. I ask to be centered." Now breathe all the qualities you prayed for fully and deeply into your center.

CHAPTER 8
THE SACRED CIRCLE

MEDICINE WHEEL:
THE SACRED CIRCLE

Ancient stone carvings and other archeological evidence suggest that the circle is one of humankind's oldest and most elemental symbols. It is no surprise, then, that stone circles have been found in the caves of our earliest ancestors and that the circle has a profound impact on the spiritual understandings and practices of peoples who live close to nature. (Some North American people refer to the sacred circle as a medicine wheel). Most primal peoples worship, raise energy, pray and celebrate within a sacred circle. Many build their dwellings in a circular manner and arrange those dwellings in a circle.

The circle is humankind's greatest symbol of perfection and wholeness. The circle's very shape speaks to us of integrity and endlessness, of unity and completion. It

113

echoes the turning and returning cycles of life and death and rebirth, of the sun and moon and seasons, of time and timelessness. The circle reminds us that there are no such things as past or future, beginning or ending, in the spirit realm. It shows us that all events, all life and everything in the universe, are connected in a perpetual flow. The circle symbolizes Earth Mother in Her roundness, fullness and abundance. No wonder that so many different native peoples have used and continue to use the circle in their rituals and ceremonies. For when we make a circle, a sacred circle, we are creating a very special and powerful space— a space where our energies become focused and strengthened, a place where we share in the mysteries of body and spirit, of time and eternity.

When we create a medicine wheel or sacred circle, we are setting aside a place that is sacred, powerful and mysterious. We are linking ourselves with all that the circle represents. The medicine wheel is an entrance way to the spirit realm, to other dimensions and times, a sacred place "between the worlds" where medicine power is raised to heal and transform for the good of all life. The sacred circle is a place where mystery, positive magic and the wild realm of possibilities meet and unfold.

The dynamic focus of the sacred circle allows us to raise and project energy and manifest it in the world. It greatly extends our medicine powers and facilitates communication with the Nature Spirits. The energy we raise helps transform us into complete and whole beings. We get in touch with the forces of nature and with our own higher self.

Because the sacred circle is so special and so powerful, whatever we do there will ultimately come back to us, magnified many times. It is important, then, that all we wish and pray for within the medicine wheel be both positive and life affirming.

Whether you create a sacred circle by yourself or together with others, you may find it helpful to go about it in a way designed to help you benefit fully from it:

How To Create A Medicine Wheel

It is actually very easy and natural to create a medicine wheel, but it is made complex by teachers, authors and hierarchical spiritual authorities who would have you believe that every sacred circle must be done one way: their way. They prescribe minute ceremonial details that must be followed exactly or, according to them, negative energy will result.

However, no one group or teacher owns the shape or power of a circle. From a tiny electron circling its nucleus to the sprawling spiral of endless galaxies, the circle is the most basic tool and the most common event in the universe. It is the primary motif of creation. The sacred circle belongs to all beings born of Earth Mother: all our lives and deaths, days and nights, winters and summers flow in an endless, repeating circle. Is it any wonder that we instinctively choose to address the most important matter in our lives, our relation to Spirit, within a sacred circle?

We can take the powerful archetypal symbol of the circle, combine it with various ceremonial elements that are common to all primal peoples and create our own sacred circle, or medicine wheel. We can mix and match these various elements differently for each circle and put our own spontaneity and imagination into it as well. Or we might find one way to do a circle that is right for us, and then always do it that way.

Before I go into all the various ways that a sacred circle might be created, let me present common elements of many native circles and medicine wheels. I want to make it clear that a sacred circle is easy, basic and resonant with the hearts of all people as humanity's oldest symbol of wholeness. The only important rule here is that everything you do within a sacred circle should be positive and life-affirming. Intent outweighs detail. The only mistake is a heart filled with bad intent. The only correct way to create a medicine wheel is with a heart filled with thankfulness and reverence towards all life. With this in mind, enjoy learning the process of raising energy in a circle.

Common Elements Of The Sacred Circle

Cleansing And Purification
Shielding From Unwanted Energies
(Some folks don't shield as long as
they cleanse and purify.)
Grounding And Centering
Creating The Circle
Calling In Positive Spirits
Raising And Sending Medicine Power
Closing The Circle

The primal peoples of the world cast their medicine wheels or sacred circles in a variety of ways. We can bring the circle into being in any way that has beauty and meaning to us. Some people sprinkle cornmeal around the circle as

116

they walk sunwise around the perimeter. Others take turns singing a sacred song around the circle. Some people draw the circle in the soil, using a staff or other ritual object. Some place stones or crystals to make the perimeter. Others simply sit or stand in a circle as each participant sings, chants or prays out loud, one at a time, around the circle in a clockwise direction. Some dance as a group—so that the dance creates the circle. Still others combine two or more of these methods or spontaneously invent methods of their own.

The various ways of creating and participating in a medicine wheel are endless. It is easier to learn how to proceed by actually doing a number of different medicine wheels than by reading an endless list of various ways to create every aspect of a sacred circle. With this in mind I offer a number of sacred circles, as exercises and verbatim transcripts of circles that I have been in. Doing all of these circles, while leaving room for your own spontaneity, is the best way to learn how to create a medicine wheel. After you've created a few medicine wheels, your own sacred imagination takes over, and you begin to wean yourself away from recipes.

A Very Simple Sacred Circle

To create your own very simple sacred circle, you might cleanse your spirit by brushing away unwanted energies with a feather. Shield by visualizing yourself surrounded by protective oak trees. Ground by touching the earth or the floor with the palms of your hands. Create the circle by taking some cornmeal and spreading it in a circle on the ground or surround yourself with a circle of crystals, twigs or any natural thing that is sacred to you. Cast this medicine wheel in a sacred manner; that is, let your actions rise intentionally from your deep feelings of respect and affection for Earth Mother.

It is good to start the circle in the east, for this is the place where the sun rises, but you can begin your circle anywhere. As you create the circle it is good to state out loud your intentions. Speak simply and from the heart. For example, "Earth Mother, I create a sacred circle today, in Your honor. May the power I raise here be for the good of all life."

When you have completed your circle, enter it. You can now raise energy by calling for aid from any positive deity, the four directions and elements, any Nature Spirit or your own ancestors. The circle simply acts as an amplifier of everything you do inside of it. When you call out to the spirit realm in a sacred circle, you will be attended to! Therefore, make sure all that you say and do is positive and life-affirming.

When you create a medicine wheel it is good to establish an atmosphere of reverence. Candles, incense or a fire in the center of the circle are common. You might place sacred objects like your medicine pouch or a crystal in the circle area. Symbolic representations of the four elements are frequently placed in or around the medicine wheel as well. For instance, a feather can be placed in the eastern quadrant of the circle to represent the element air; a candle in the southern section represents fire; a bowl of water or a sea shell in the western section represents the element water; a container of earth or a stone in the northern quadrant of the medicine wheel would represent earth.

Your sacred circle can be indoors or outdoors, but it should be a quiet place where you will not be interrupted. You can sit or stand during any part of the medicine wheel. If you are moved to dance or lie down during any part of the medicine wheel, do so.

A Very Simple Medicine Wheel

__Purify with the spirit cleansing powers of green plants__ by lighting a cedar incense stick and waving it around yourself.

__Shield__ by visualizing yourself surrounded by a circle of white light.

__Ground__ by breathing deeply until you feel calm and centered.

__Create the medicine wheel__ by walking the perimeter of a circle clockwise in a sacred manner, with a feeling of reverence for Earth Mother in your heart. Once you've made the circle, enter it.

__Call in positive spirits__ by addressing one or more spirit helpers to assist you in raising the medicine power: your ancestors, the four directions, a deity, your animal spirit guardian or any positive spirit beings. Speak to them simply. For example: "Grandmother, enter my medicine wheel and help me raise powerful energy."

__Raise medicine power__ by invoking one or more of the invited spirits into yourself. For example, you might call upon Wolf Spirit to fill you with loyalty and courage. Or you could pray to your deceased grandmother to help or guide you. Or you might ask the Great Spirit to save all endangered animals. You might pray, ask, invoke, visual-

ize or even dance and sing—or just talk to the spirit realm.
You might also sit quietly and see if there is a message for you from the spirit realm. <u>**Close the circle**</u> *by giving thanks to all the spirits you called upon.*

Simple Medicine Wheel With More Explanations

<u>**Cleanse and purify**</u> *an area indoors or outdoors where the circle is to be. Do this by waving the smoke from any cleansing herb around the area. Now wave the smoke around yourself while asking for purification, e.g., "Spirits of Cedar, cleanse me that I might enter sacred space with a pure heart."*

<u>**Shield**</u> *by addressing Earth Mother, saying something from the heart, such as, "Earth Mother, I come here for the good of all life and I invite only good here."*

<u>**Ground and center**</u> *by touching the earth (or the floor) and imagining your body growing roots into the earth, like a tree. Feel yourself draw energy from the earth through your roots.*

<u>**Create the circle**</u> *by casting cornmeal, flower petals, bird seed or any other appropriate thing in a clockwise circle while walking the perimeter of a circle of any size (as long as it is large enough for you to get inside of). Begin in the east and walk around once, ending in the east. The east is a good place to begin, for this is where the sun rises. As you walk slowly around the circle, hold a feeling of reverence in your heart. You might say something out loud as well, for instance, "Earth Mother, I create a medicine wheel in a sacred manner, with reverence for all life in my heart." When you have walked the circle once around, enter it.*

The Sacred Circle

__Call in positive spirits__ by calling on the four cardinal directions to enter the medicine wheel and help you raise medicine power. Do this in your own words or say,

> *East, West, South, North*
> *In sacred space I call you forth.*
> *Bring your power and your grace,*
> *Live within this sacred place.*

You might also call any other positive spirits or deities into your circle to bring their power, love and protection as you stand in sacred space.

__Raise medicine power__ with rhythmic movement accompanied by spoken or sung prayers. Shake your rattle or beat your drum, allowing yourself to move as you do so. As you let yourself go into the mood and movement, you will probably find the tempo increasing. As the energy is raised with rhythm, begin to say or chant your need, your wish, your prayer. Sing, chant or pray spontaneously, from the depths of your being. Let your whole body become a moving prayer that rises from the deepest part of you. Let your emotions carry the prayer to Earth Mother and Sun Father. If you cry or laugh, yell, sing or dance fervently, that is fine. This type of moving prayer has much power for it sends the prayer forth with great energy. Let yourself go and let the mystery power work through you.

When the energy peaks, let yourself relax totally, perhaps lying down on the ground. Wait to see if any of the spirits you invited into the circle respond to or communicate with you in any way.

__Close the circle__ by thanking the spirits you have

121

called upon and let it go at that. Or you may undo the circle more formally by moving around it counter-clockwise.

A Simple Group Medicine Wheel

We cleanse *by sprinkling water on each other and asking for purification as we are sprinkled.*

Dolfyn: "Spirits of Water, cleanse me of my worries and fears that I may enter sacred space."

Coyote: "Water Spirits, cleanse me of my timidity that I may share energy with others."

Otter: "Spirits of Water, bathe my heart in good feelings, bathe my mind with good thoughts."

We shield *by visualizing white light surrounding our circle.*

We ground *by holding hands around the circle, and breathing deeply together for a few moments.*

We create the circle *by passing a crow feather around the circle clockwise. As each person holds the feather, he or she speaks a brief sentence about the spirit force that they bring to the circle.*

Dolfyn: "In laughter and joy I create sacred space."

Coyote: "With gentleness and calmness I create this medicine wheel."

Otter: "In love and hope I create this circle."

We invite positive spirits *to help us raise the medicine power by invoking the animal spirits associated with the four directions.*

We face the East and move and call like Eagle and other birds.

We then face South and move and make sounds like Lion and Coyote.

The Sacred Circle

Then we face West and move and call like Dolphin and other sea beings.

Finally, we face North and move and call and become like Buffalo, Polar Bear and other polar animals.

__We raise medicine power__ in conjunction with the powers of Fire Spirits and Tree Spirits. We pick up dead leaves from the ground and hold them over our hearts as we charge the leaves with the things we wish for, by visualizing the desires of our hearts going into the leaves.

Then, one at a time, we throw the leaf into the fire and state a brief prayer. As the leaf burns, the medicine prayer is made manifest and rises to the spirit powers on sacred smoke. During this part of the ritual the group chants:

> *Smoke and Flame, Smoke and Flame*
> *Protect all that's wild and untame.*
> *Smoke and Fire, Smoke and Fire*
> *Grant to us our heart's desire!*

__We close the circle__ by giving thanks to the spirits we called upon.

Now that you have experienced a few sacred circles you can begin creating your own medicine wheels.

With this in mind, I now present a variety of ways to do each step of the circle. I am limited by space to just a few of the many different ways you can do them. You are limited only by imagination. After you have created many circles, using the various methods presented here, you will find that you can create a unique and spontaneous circle, allowing your sacred imagination and Earth Mother to guide you.

Begin by cleansing or ritually purifying yourself. The act of removing negative energies by smudging with smoke, sprinkling with water or waving objects such as crystals around you (or around each other if it is a group circle) also affirms your willingness to step aside from mundane concerns and enter the dimensions of sacred mystery. Other ways to purify ritually include brushing off unwanted energies with a feather or breathing unwanted energies into a container of water or earth. You might also develop your own unique methods of ritual purification.

As you symbolically cleanse, you might speak aloud to the spirits of the element you are cleansing with and ask for specific or general purification. For instance, if you cleanse with water, you might say something like, "Spirits of Water, wash away my mundane fears and doubts that I might enter sacred space."

The next process to be done before creating a medicine wheel is shielding. You shield to remind yourself what you are trying to accomplish and to protect yourself from unwanted energies. A very simple way to do this is to visualize yourself surrounded by white light. You might also say something to this effect: "I am a being of pure white light, surrounded by a circle of pure white light. Only good can come to me. Only good can flow from me. Only good can be here." Some people shield by bathing themselves and their surroundings with love. Others shield by calling upon their Spirit Guardians to shield them. Others shield by reminding themselves, Earth Mother and other spirits why they are creating a sacred circle and what kind

The Sacred Circle

of energy they hope to attract. Again, try these various modes of shielding and then begin to create your own.

Grounding and centering are the next steps in preparing ourselves for the medicine wheel. There are many ways to do this. Some of them are: Breathe deeply and slowly, until you feel calm and centered. Touch the earth or even lie down upon Her for awhile, feeling Her support and love flowing into you. If you are circling with others, it is very grounding simply to hold each other's hands or hug each other. Tree hugging is also quite grounding. Finally, you might imagine the earth's energy flowing up into you, as if you had roots like a tree.

Now you are ready to create the medicine wheel. Remember, this is usually done in a sunwise (clockwise) direction, for this is the direction of increasing energy. You can begin the circle anywhere, but it is usually begun in the east or the north. The east is a good place to begin creating the circle, for that is the place the sun rises each new day and a good place for beginnings.

Once you've made the circle, enter it. By creating a medicine wheel in a sacred manner, you have created a powerful container that will focus and enhance any energy you now raise. But humans cannot and should not work with the powerful medicine of a circle alone. Therefore we call in, invite or invoke positive spirits and deities into the medicine wheel. It is customary for many to call in the spirits of the four directions and elements at this time. You can do this simply by turning to a direction and addressing the spirits of each one aloud, speaking sincerely and simply. For example, you might turn to face east, raise your arms toward the east and say, "Spirits of the East, element of Air, powers of illumination and new beginnings, enter this sacred circle and bring your blessings." Then turn south, raise your arms and say, "Spirits of the South, element of Fire, place of warmth and passion, bring your spirit powers to this sacred circle." "Spirits of West, element of Water, of cleansing, healing and consecration, bring these blessings to this sacred circle." "Spirits of North, element of Earth, place of quiet and wisdom and deep inner knowing, bring these mysteries to this sacred circle." It is best, however, to address the spirits of the four directions in your own heartfelt words and to wean yourself as quickly as possible from reciting prayers and invocations created by anyone else.

Now is also the time to call upon any other spirit helpers you will need to assist you in raising the medicine power. You might ask a deity that you worship, an ancestor, or a beloved friend or pet who is now in the spirit realm to join you. Some people invoke the spirit of a great person such as Ghandi or Martin Luther King, Jr. to enter the circle and bring their blessings and their power. Others invite the Nature Spirits they love most or their Nature Spirit Guardians. There is no limit to the number of good spirits you might call into your circle. You might address each of these spirits aloud, speaking sincerely and simply, or you might invoke the spirits by dancing as them, emulating them or becoming them momentarily. For example, if you are inviting the spirits of trees into the circle, you might wave your arms in the air like branches and leaves waving in the breeze. On the other hand, some folks just call in the four directions and leave it at that.

After you have done the above, you are prepared to

The Sacred Circle

call upon the energies of the universe, to raise medicine power. As you can see from the medicine wheels presented in this section and from the numerous examples of various ways to raise medicine power throughout this book, you can raise medicine power in many different ways. In fact, there are as many ways to raise medicine power in a sacred circle as there are forces in nature with which to raise that power. We enact, ritualize or make graphic our wishes to show the spirit realm (and our own magical selves) exactly what we wish to manifest. The spirits of the universe understand and respond to symbols, pictures, song, rhyme, dance and emotions better than just words alone. When we combine any of these methods with the forces and elements of nature, the medicine power is greatly enhanced.

For instance, combine spoken prayer with Fire by speaking the prayer into the flames and smoke of a candle flame or wood fire. The Spirits of Smoke and Fire then take your prayer up to the spirits of the universe. Another way to raise medicine power in conjunction with Fire Spirits is to write or draw your prayer or wish on a piece of paper and then burn the paper while asking that the Fire Spirits transform the energy into a prayer that ascends to the four corners of the universe on sacred smoke. When we raise medicine power in a group circle, we can have one person stand, sit or lie in the middle of the circle and pray out loud while the rest of us shake our rattles over and around that person to raise the power as we pray for that one person's wish. Or the group can all raise energy together for a common prayer with rhythm, movement, chants, and so forth. This type of moving, rhythmic, chanting meditation facilitates entrance to the mystery realm. Chants can be very simple, for example:

"The Earth is our mother and we are the Earth.
We steward Her, for She gave us birth."

After the energy is raised with the chant, the group might then all put their hands on the ground and visualize green healing light surrounding the earth. Or send feelings of love from their hearts into their hands to heal Earth Mother. Or visualize the streams and oceans running clean and clear again.

Throughout this book there are numerous examples of how to raise medicine power in conjunction with the forces of nature. You might begin using any of these ways in your circle until you develop your own ways to raise medicine power inside a circle.

You can close the circle by thanking the spirits you have called upon, and let it go at that. Or you may undo the circle more formally by moving around it counter-clockwise, three times, literally undoing the circle you created.

As you can see, a sacred circle can be as simple or as elaborate as you and your companions choose to make it. The only limit is the caution to work for the benefit all beings and to always pray for the web of life which sustains you and all of us.

A Very Simple Review Of A Very Simple Circle

Cleanse *by smudging yourself with an incense stick.*
Shield *by visualizing white light around yourself.*
Ground *by breathing deeply until you are centered.*

The Sacred Circle

__Walk once around the circle sunwise (clockwise)__ in a sacred manner, beginning and ending in the east.

__Get into the circle and invite in the four directions__ by turning to each direction and calling it into the circle simply and from your heart.

__Invite other positive deities or spirits into the circle__ to lend their help and power.

__Raise medicine power __ (or pray for that which you need).

__Pray for the healing of Earth Mother.__

__Close the circle __ by thanking the directions and other spirit beings invited in.

The new and full moons, the spring and fall equinoxes, the summer and winter solstices are all very powerful times for medicine wheels. But you can create one any time you want.

After you have created and participated in a number of medicine wheels, you might try a spontaneous sacred circle. If it is a group circle, you might discuss the focus of the medicine wheel to get a loose idea of how it will unfold, but leave much room for spontaneity. Or you might simply let the entire experience be guided by the Great Mystery—with no conscious planning at all. This usually works best with folks who have experienced many medicine wheels. If you keep in mind that chaos and hilarity are also a part of the great sacred mystery, a totally spontaneous sacred circle can be a very powerful and transforming experience. At the very least, a totally spontaneous group medicine wheel is always a graphic lesson in letting go of control and allowing the mystery power to unfold (or not) as it will (or won't).

Shamanic Wisdom

Paradoxically, it is often in or around the spaces where "nothing" seems to be happening that the greatest medicine and magic occurs!

Here is what unfolded at a spontaneous spring equinox circle of friends who had circled together many times before.

A Spontaneous Spring Equinox Circle

We meet indoors on a cold rainy night.

__We cleanse__ by opening the door a crack and one at a time, each person bathes themselves in the cold, sharp March wind. As we do this, we ask Winter to purify our hearts.

Owl: "Wind and Rain, cleanse me of that which has kept me isolated and lonely these last few months."

Coyote: " Sharp Wind, blow away my doubts and cynicism."

Dolfyn: "March wind, I feel your chilly cleansing as you roar by me. Take my fears with you!"

__We shield__ by visualizing a protective circle of Tree Spirits surrounding us.

__We ground__ by touching each other. We give a brief shoulder massage to each other simultaneously around the circle.

__Then we begin to create the medicine wheel__ by speaking in a sacred manner, clockwise around the circle, about our intentions tonight.

Owl: "We raise medicine power tonight to help Earth Mother wake up fully, and burst forth in the glorious springtime of Her cycle."

Coyote: "Spring is born again, and our blessed

The Sacred Circle

Earth Mother awakens from Her long sleep."

Dolfyn: "Earth Mother awakens to bless us with Her renewal, Her abundance, Her promise. We celebrate with Her tonight."

<u>We call in the four directions and other positive spirits</u> by dancing around the circle as them. We do this all simultaneously. So at any time, one of us dances as the East, while another dances as Sun Father, while still another dances as her grandmother who lives in the spirit realm.

<u>Then we all get under a blanket and whisper in the dark what the winter meant for us and also how glad we are that spring is here.</u> We speak as if we are the earth (as, indeed, we all are).

Owl: "I harbored life deep within, all winter long. Now, at long last, I'm ready to awaken."

Coyote: "I was often cold and lonely, but deep warm secrets lived within my heart. I am ready to wake up."

Dolfyn: "I slept and dreamed all curled in a ball. I'm ready now to awaken."

<u>Now we awaken the spring within each of us and within Earth Mother.</u>

Owl rocks Coyote in her arms and says "You are the earth, and you are born anew." Coyote opens his eyes, smiles and stretches. Coyote tickles Dolfyn who quickly says, "O.K., I'm up." Dolfyn massages Owl's feet and says, "Wake up, wake up, it's time to shine." We all throw off the blanket and dance in a circle, beating our drums, singing, laughing and joking, for this is a time to be joyous. When the energy peaks, we each send a silent prayer for the

healing of Earth Mother.
    Then we feast on fruits and bread as we sit in the circle and speak of our plans and dreams for the spring.
    We close the circle by giving thanks to the spirits we called upon.

Sacred circles can also be created informally and with no preparation. For example, some people simply visualize a circle of white light surrounding themselves and pray or call upon the spirits mentally. Other informal circles will suggest themselves from your surroundings.

Informal Sacred Circle

In your yard or on your deck or porch, gather gifts from nature, such as rocks, sea shells, twigs and so forth. Arrange them in a sacred manner by placing them sunwise and stating your intent as you lay the objects down. for example: "Earth Mother, I create a sacred space in Your essence and in Your name." Inside this permanent circle, you may meditate, pray, do yoga, do other spiritual things— or you might simply sit inside the circle to read, write or contemplate life. Be sure, however, that you do only positive things inside the circle.

Some people permanently encircle their gardens and other special areas of their yards. Others draw with a twig or visualize a circle around their houses, cars or places of business. Some people round out the corners of their rooms by arranging the furniture in a circular manner or by placing crystals and other stones in the corners. Still others make a permanent medicine wheel around their houses with

The Sacred Circle

stones, shells or twigs.

There are many ways to work with the powerful energies of the circle. You might place a small circle of natural objects on an indoor altar or on a desk or table. Then write down what you wish for and put the paper in the circle. Or you might simply walk in a circle around your house or around your room, asking for protection or a wish to be granted. When I feel the need for protection, I often visualize a circle of oak trees surrounding myself. I then pray to the Oak Spirits for protection. The simplest circle prayer involves only drawing a circle on a piece of paper and writing the wish upon it. If you bury the paper in the earth on the full moon, while visualizing and stating the prayer, the medicine power will be enhanced.

Finally, whenever you are in a natural place, you can draw a circle in the earth with a twig or visualize the place surrounded by a circle of white light in order to protect that place. (Do not move rocks into a circle because we must never disturb the natural beauty of a place. Earth Mother situated the rocks just where they should be.) But we can make a circle of twigs, leaves or small pebbles that we find on the ground. When I am in a natural place I often walk a sunwise circle around a large area while I meditate, visualize and pray for the protection of that place.

No matter why we create or use a sacred circle, it reminds us always of the healing wholeness that comes from our intimacy with our Earth Mother and of the security we have in the great medicine wheel of Her embrace.

CHAPTER 9

SUN FATHER, MOON MOTHER

SUN FATHER

The sun, like every other part of the Creation, is alive, a being aware of itself and its place in the universe. Just as rocks, water, air, earth, fire and all natural things on earth are alive and conscious, so is the sun. Every natural thing in the heavens and on earth is a living conscious part of the whole. And just as we can turn to the energies of animals, trees and minerals for help, so we can pray to the sun, too—with this difference: as a major aspect of creative power that holds our section of the universe in being, the sun is more than an expression of energy; it is a primary source and symbol of all our powers here on Earth Mother.

In many shamanic traditions Sun Father, or the Sun God, is the male aspect of the Great Spirit. Sun Father is the God aspect of our solar system. Earth and Moon are the Goddess aspect. Sun Father holds Earth Mother in the warm embrace of His gravitational field. Earth and Sun are

135

two great cosmic beings in relationship. It is out of this loving relationship that life is born and nurtured on earth, for our Sun Father holds our Earth Mother at the exact distance necessary to ensure life on earth.

This manifestation of the Great Spirit speaks to us of enormous energy. Sun Father bathes all life in His warmth, protection and life-giving glow. He fills us with strength and power and teaches us the wise and good use of that power. Just as Sun Father's life-giving light inspires the seedling to grow towards it, so does Sun Father urge our own growth toward the light and the good. Sun Father, living in the heavens, bestows on us the gifts of enlightenment and transcendence. His radiance inspires us to rise above the limits of our own mindsets and to reach beyond the mundane world, striving towards the light in our spiritual quest. Nevertheless, as Earth Mother's consort, He shows us how to return our transcendent insights to the earth in service and affection.

Just as a sunny day fills us with optimism and lifts our spirits, so does Sun Father bring contentment, gaiety, pleasure and positive feelings to His children. Sun Father is also associated with happiness, moral excellence, analytical skill, open-handed abundance and virtue. Pray to Him for these attributes. Sun Father inspires honesty, integrity and strength of will. He ennobles all who pray to Him with intelligence, knowledge, clarity of perception, luck, prosperity and cheerfulness. He fosters what is best of our own male aspect, encouraging us to be bold in vision, energetic in action, generous and protective towards all creatures. And just as Sun Father shares His life force with all of His children, so does He inspire us to shine our own loving light upon others.

Sun Father Invocation

Sit or lie down in full sunlight...Feel His loving warmth relax you and lighten your spirit...Begin breathing slowly and deeply. With each breath that you breathe in, visualize sunlight entering through the top of your head and filling your body with a golden glow...Let this radiance flow through you, dissolving all negative thoughts...Feel the glow light your heart and purify it of all negative feelings. Let the light flow into your body until every part of you is brimming with this shimmering radiance...When you are totally filled with light, feel it overflowing from your heart to all the creatures of the earth. While Sun Father continues to fill you with His glow, project the light from your heart to surround Earth Mother Herself with a golden halo of protection and love.

Sun Father can be honored at any time. He is worshipped at His solar peaks, and He is honored at these times by Earth-Spirited people everywhere. At this time, any medicine power you raise is greatly enhanced. I offer these solar ceremonies as a way for a beginner to get started. Feel free to change them in any way that has meaning and beauty to you or create your own spontaneous ceremonies. These ceremonies follow the seasons of the northern hemisphere. Your section of the world or even of this hemisphere might vary greatly from the norm. For example, the big seasonal event in northern California might be the coming of the rain in the fall, as opposed to the coming of the cold. Adjust your solar ceremonies accordingly.

Shamanic Wisdom

Winter Solstice: December 20-23

On the longest night and shortest day of the year we celebrate hope and happiness in the midst of darkness and cold. Sun Father seems to be weakening and dying all winter long. And yet, on the day after this long night, He is reborn and begins to grow strong again. Thus the theme of rebirth is the essence of this celebration.

This is the time to acknowledge all within ourselves that has grown cold and dark. As we light the Solstice fire, we make a prayer for the rebirth, in our hearts, of warmth and light.

The ancient, Earth-Spirited native peoples of Europe called this time Yule. Many of the themes and symbols of Yule were borrowed by the Christians, who conquered and converted the nature folk by force. Holly, mistletoe, the Yule log, the evergreen tree and the idea of redemption and rebirth out of the death of winter are essential features of this ancient European shamanic Sun Celebration.

The Hopi call this time Soyal or Soyalangwul. The literal translation of this word is "establishing life anew for all the world." It is also a common shamanic belief that we can aid, help and participate with nature, and all the universe, through our rituals. The Hopis fast and concentrate at Winter Solstice on lending Sun Father strength and direction to get through this long night and to be reborn in the new dawn of hope. In our ritual actions on this night we, too, are midwives to the rebirth of the sun.

Sun Father, Moon Mother

Winter Solstice Ceremony

On the night of the Solstice place a sprig of evergreen in the center of the medicine wheel. If you can do this outside, have a small fire in the center as well. If your circle is indoors, make use of a fireplace or put candles in the center of the circle. After you have created the medicine wheel, while your fire is still small, sit down and feel the cold. The tiny fire symbolizes Sun Father's weakest moment. Now think of the fires within yourself that you or the world have let die down: your trust, perhaps, or your sense of creativity and fun, your confidence or your courage... Close your eyes and feel the cold within and without, for it is time to transform all that. The great medicine wheel turns tonight, and all the universe is aligned for a return to warmth and hope. The fire of life will burn anew—within and without.

Now speak aloud in a strong voice, "Sun Father, in the midst of gloom, of winter death, You are reborn as is my (courage or whatever). Then place a piece of wood on the fire to symbolize the rebirth of warmth and light. If you cannot light a fire, then light candles in the center of the circle. (If you are performing this ritual alone you might put many pieces of wood on the fire, naming each quality that you are rebirthing. In a group, each person puts one piece of wood on, or lights one candle, while stating that which is to be reborn this night.)

As the fire grows stronger, let yourself feel your heart grow warm, your positive feelings begin to flow. Also think of Sun Father's increase and the promise of spring and summer.

Shamanic Wisdom

Begin to drum or rattle, and move your body in a joyous dance to all of this. If spontaneous words or chants or prayers come, say them. The energy you put into this helps Sun Father to be born again and helps the fire within your spirit to re-kindle as well. When you are finished, close the medicine wheel and give thanks.

Initiation Time

Early February is the time for initiation and purification for many Earth-Spirited peoples of this hemisphere. The European shamanic peoples celebrate this occasion on February 2 and call it (depending on their particular locale and tradition) Candlemas, Imbolc, Brigid or Lady Day. The Hopis call it Powamu and celebrate it at this time of the year.

The great medicine wheel turns again as the days lengthen and Sun Father grows stronger. So it is time to celebrate and acknowledge the waxing of the light, the warming of Earth Mother. As the seeds stir deep within Her womb, our Great Mother begins to awaken from Her long winter's sleep.

Just as the increasing light has inspired the seeds within the earth to awaken, so is this a time of inspiration, individuation, initiation and purification of ourselves.

We build a medicine wheel and light a fire (or candles) at this time to symbolize the waxing (increasing)light. We first look at our past behavior, and we state aloud how we can improve it. This purification helps us grow and also helps the earth to renew itself as well. From the central fire we then light our own individual candle, stating aloud that for which we seek initiation or inspiration in ourselves.

Sun Father, Moon Mother

Spring Equinox: March 20-23

The great wheel turns yet again, and we celebrate spring's return. Life is reborn as the tiny plants push through the earth and Earth Mother throws off the bonds of winter. We are now filled with the hope and expectation of spring's promise.

At equinox the daylight and the dark are of exactly equal length. This is a time to bring new balance and harmony into our lives and to throw off anything which keeps us bound—a time to liberate our spirits.

The European shamanic peoples call this time Ostara or Eostar. Again, many of the symbols and themes of Easter were taken from the conquered nature people; the rabbit and the egg, for example, symbolized the fertility of Earth Mother.

Bring a pot of earth and a seed into the medicine wheel. Meditate on something in yourself that needs nurturing—something that was a tiny seed in the cold earth and that is now ready to begin its growth.

We also concentrate on balance within our medicine wheel. We meditate upon that which we need to bring into balance within ourselves at this time. We then celebrate winter's end by making joyous rhythm and moving our bodies freely as we call, sing, chant and express our love of life and our freedom from winter's harsh restrictions. We call out our wishes and our desires to the four corners of the universe.

Shamanic Wisdom

The Flowering Time

Early May is a time to celebrate the full return of spring from the death of winter. Sun Father envelops Earth Mother in His soft warmth at this season. And all of Earth Mother's children respond to the great mystery of love, romance, desire, mating and fertility. At this time we notice young life is everywhere. And something young awakens within our hearts no matter how old we are.

On May 1, European shamanic peoples celebrate Beltane. They traditionally light a Beltane fire at this time and leap the flames as they make a wish or prayer on the waxing light.

If you can create your spring medicine wheel outdoors, then it is good to do it in a garden. For this is a time to dance and leap about in nature, just as the roe buck leaps with joy to welcome the full flowering of spring. Create a large medicine wheel and leap over the young seedlings that grow within your circle. This energizes our green brothers and sisters and also shows them how high to grow. Light a candle and place it in the middle of the circle. (I have been in circles where a bonfire is put in the middle of the circle to leap, but only the young, brave, agile people in the circle could leap it. I think it is better, and safer, to use candles or a smaller fire so that all members of the circle can participate.) Then each member of the circle yells aloud their prayer as they jump the candle. The higher you jump the more energy you put into the prayer. As each person completes their jump, the others shake their rattles, beat their drums, hoot and holler their applause for this great leap into life, into desire and into the warm promise of the summer to come.

This is the most auspicious time of the year to pray for romantic love. Beware that if you leap the flame on May 1 while fervently asking aloud for romantic love, you will very probably get it. I know this from experience. And once you have obtained anything through the use of medicine power in a sacred circle, it is not all that easy to get rid of! Fair warning.

Summer Solstice: June 20-23

On the longest day and shortest night of the year, Sun Father is at His full strength. His warmth has caused the young life to grow and flourish. And yet tomorrow He will wane, and begin to die again. Tomorrow Earth Mother and all Her children must face the coming darkness of winter.

We join in the dance once more, to help turn the great medicine wheel of our Sun Father. We celebrate the sacred fulfillment of spring's promise. For today the sun is bright and warm, and this is our time to shine as well.

The Hopis call this time Niman Kachina. European Shamanic peoples call it Litha.

The focus of this medicine wheel is a final celebration of Sun Father's glory. We sing and dance, feast and shine. For even though we know our sacred Sun Father must die tomorrow, we also realize that He will be reborn at Winter Solstice. We affirm that death is not permanent and that life and hope will be reborn at Winter Solstice.

Shamanic Wisdom

First Harvest

In early August we reap Earth Mother's first harvest. European shamanic peoples celebrate this time on August 1 as Lammas or Lughnasad. The Hopis celebrate it in mid-August as Chu Tiva.

The tiny seedlings that we planted in spring have matured and the ancient promise of our Sun Father and Earth Mother has been kept. At this season we give our thanks and express our wonder at the sustenance from the earth. As we hold the first fruit of summer in our hands, we look up at Sun Father and then down at Earth Mother in thanks for the great mystery that created this food for us. And at this time we celebrate the warmth and light of late summer, knowing full well that winter is ever closer.

Bring fruits into the medicine wheel. Since the main harvest is not in yet, we concentrate on completion. Before we eat the fruit, we hold it to our hearts and visualize, speak about and project something we have worked for that is near completion that we would like to see safely to harvest. Next, we give thanks for the promise kept as we eat the fruits of first harvest.

Finally, we meditate on a promise that we have made, and we vow to fulfill that promise at this season.

Fall Equinox: September 20-23

Again we give thanks at this second harvest celebration. Night and day are again of equal length and the universe is in perfect balance. At this time we concentrate on balancing our spirits.

European shamanic peoples celebrate Mabon at this

Sun Father, Moon Mother

time. The Hopis observe Lakon in late September or early October, when the corn is harvested.

This time marks the main harvest celebration of thanks. We planted seeds of hope and renewal in the earth and also within ourselves during the spring. Now is the time to harvest our hope.

Bring healthy, simple foods into the medicine wheel: fruits and nuts. This is the time to harvest our dreams. Think about the things you have worked hard for all year, the things you are now ready to harvest. Write or draw them on a piece of paper. Hold the paper over your heart as you affirm your readiness for fulfillment. Then toss the paper on the fire or burn it in a metal bowl. The heat and flame transform the wish to pure energy, and the smoke takes the medicine prayer up to the Creator.

Now meditate upon the coming season and focus upon what inner attitude you need to bring into balance to face the winter.

Finally feast and give thanks for the great bounty of Earth Mother.

Late Fall

The European Earth-Spirited peoples celebrate Samhain on October 31. In the late fall the Hopis observe Owaqlt. This is the final harvest festival. We feast again and give thanks, for we have planted and harvested our dreams.

Now is the time to express our happiness and our contentment in order to sustain our spirits for the long winter ahead. We face the great mystery of life that dies again each fall with courage and a sense of completion. We

Shamanic Wisdom

face this ancient mystery together in ceremony and celebration. We remind each other that life is born anew after the cold winter's sleep. We remind each other that death is not permanent, but life is eternal.

At this time of the year, the separation between our world and the spirit world is thinnest. This is a good time to communicate with loved ones who have gone to the spirit world. And because the veil between the worlds is lifted more than usual at this time, it is also an auspicious time for all divination such as Tarot, I Ching, seeing the future, palm reading, crystal gazing and so forth. This is also a very good time to go on inner trance journeys to the spirit realm.

Bring autumn leaves and other symbols of this season into the circle. Also bring a divination tool such as Tarot cards, the I Ching or a gazing crystal.

Pick up a dead and fallen leaf, hold it to your heart, and call, through the leaf, to a loved one who has passed on to the spirit world. Put a message to them into the leaf, send them your love and ask them to be with you and communicate with you. You might also pray to them for a wish to be granted or for guidance, for now that they are of spirit, they have spirit powers. Begin to speak to or about your loved one. You can do this whether you are circling alone or with a group. When you are through speaking, gently place the leaf back on the earth. Listen for a message from your loved one.

A good way to do a brief divination in a group is for each person silently to ask a question to which they need an answer and then to select one Tarot card from the deck without looking at it. Then each person can tell the group which card they picked, and the group can help decipher the

146

meaning. If you are circling alone, you might pick one card or do an entire layout.

If you have brought a crystal to gaze into, you might ask your question and then hold the crystal up to the fire or candle flame in the middle of the medicine wheel, turning it this way or that until a picture or answer emerges in the crystal. Again, if you are in a group, the participants might help each other interpret the message.

MOON

Shamans have great mystery power because they align themselves with the forces of the universe. For those of us who live on Earth, Moon is one of the most constant and influential forces. Moon represents feminine strengths and abilities. She is soft and reflective, yet filled with power.

We are linked to the Moon in many ways because we are a part of the Earth, and Earth and Moon are in relationship. The seas rise and ebb to the rhythms of Her cycles, so all the beings born from the ancient womb of the sea, including ourselves, have a very special relationship with Her. Just as Moon pulls on the tides of Grandmother Ocean, so does She tug at our very blood. After all, our mother's womb was an ocean, and our blood is very similar in chemical composition to sea water.

To gain shamanic wisdom and power, therefore, we must attune our lives to Moon's phases. It is a good thing to create a medicine wheel during the new and full moons, especially, because these are the times of biological high tide, when the mystery power flows strong for all earth's creatures. The circle should focus on the energies of that time. So one might invoke abundance during the full moon circle or hope during the new moon circle. Full and new moon are also the two most powerful times in the month to raise medicine power, to pray, to invoke and to do positive visualizations and affirmations—even if you don't do them in a circle.

Those who live close to nature honor Moon in all Her phases. Go outside often beneath Moon and bathe in Her light. At Her various phases, She fills us with various energies.

Full Moon

At Her fullest, Moon's energies foster abundance, completion, sensuality, nurturing and bonding. It is the time when the universe is aligned for romance, high energy, fulfillment, fruition, sexuality, good luck, mothering, caring and attracting love.

Earth-Spirited people acknowledge the full moon, for it is the best time of the month to pray, raise energy and celebrate life. In this phase, Moon represents the mothering aspect of the Great Spirit, bathing the earth with abundant love. She is called Moon Mother at this time by many shamanic cultures, and it is on Her night that we celebrate the gifts we have been given. We give thanks on this night and ask that this abundance be given to all beings so that the earth may be healed and balance may be restored to the universe.

In honor to the Mother aspect of creation, we who follow a shamanic path celebrate on this night by creating a medicine wheel and dancing in joyous celebration of life. For it is the mothering aspect of the Great Spirit that nurtures, loves and creates life. Many people find that the full moon invites them to express their prayers in energy-filled ways—singing, dancing, chanting, drumming and making music. These are good ways to give thanks and good ways to ask for whatever you and your close relations may need. Your own medicine powers will be greatly enhanced by the moon power at Her fullest surging.

All romantic undertakings are heightened at the full moon. This is the best time of the month to pray for romance or to plan a romantic evening. This is also the best night of the month to pray for prosperity, good luck and success.

This is the asking time, when the wild realm of possibilities opens and prayers are fulfilled. So never let a full moon go by without at least praying for something you need. This is the highest energy period of the month for raising medicine power in any way. This is a time of biological high tide, as the full moon pulls on our blood and our own energies peak.

Whether or not you create a medicine wheel at this time, you can still beat your drum, shake your rattle, sing, dance or in some other way acknowledge your praise of Her, the great Mother of Creation, and Her symbolic representative, the Moon, in Her fullness.

New Moon

We meditate on the full moon as the Mother of Creation in Her ripe maturity; in the new moon, however, we honor Her in Her Maiden aspect. The new moon is a time of regeneration, renewal, creativity, hope, new beginnings, new projects, new relationships, innocence, rebirth and liberation.

The Maiden or young woman aspect of the Great Mother of Creation is reflected in the new moon. We connect with this face of the Great Mother as the Protectress of women and children and the embodiment of youthful freedom. The new moon reflects Corn Maiden in the American Indian tradition, or the Dianic or Artemis archetype of the Great Goddess in the western shamanic tradition. You might consider this aspect of the Great Spirit as a Goddess or as a symbol of independence and freedom. Corn Maiden and Her visual manifestation as the new moon protects all of the wild creatures and their habitats. Pray to the Maiden at the new moon, for at this time Her energies can be invoked and manifested within yourself.

The time of the new moon, in many shamanic traditions, is the time for renewed hope, rebirth of creativity and the time to begin any new project. The new moon is likewise a time for hope and support for those of us who seek freedom. The Goddess in Her Maiden aspect grants fortitude and strength to those who quest for liberation of any kind; spiritual, emotional or mental. It is She—the wild, free and unfettered Maiden of New Beginnings, the Lady of the Wild Things—who awakens the spirit of freedom in the hearts of all living beings.

Dark Moon

In this part of the moon's cycle, the Ancient Grandmother side of the Great Mother shows Herself in all Her wisdom. In Her dark moon aspect she bestows the gifts of intuitive knowing, serenity, psychic abilities, understanding of death, meditation, deep magical dreams and insight into our own subconscious minds. Pray to Her at this time for the wisdom of the Ancients and the peace that comes with that wisdom. During this time She invites us to turn inward and, through meditation and intuitive insights, to perceive with Her the wholeness of life—from birth to death to rebirth. This is the time to go within, to be silent, to trance, to dream.

The dark of the moon is the time that the psychic arts flourish and deep, deep memories of distant times and ancient ways stir. Our psychic powers flow, and the wisdom to use those powers wisely and well are granted us at this time. This is a good time for divination, such as Tarot, I Ching, and crystal gazing. Tap your inner powers at this deep and secret time, to fathom the great mysteries.

Moon Greeting

When you see the moon in the sky for the first time each night, stand firmly on the ground, raise your arms in an arc that represents Her crescent, and kiss your palms three times to Her. Show your respect, in this greeting, for all that is female in the world. Then speak to Moon and establish a relationship with Her. She will teach you great medicine and mystery. Ask Her to open your eyes to the Moonlight Vision, that you may see the past and the future, that you may see with intuitive wisdom and insight. Ask Her to teach you to see through the darkness into the great mysteries. Breathe deeply and allow the Moon Goddess in to open your heart to the female aspect of nurturing love and gentleness. Then feel yourself bathed in the Moon glow of Her love.

The new moon waxes (grows bigger) until it be- comes full. Right after the full moon, the moon begins to wane (grow smaller) until the next new moon, when it starts waxing again. The waxing moon is an outward time, a time to raise medicine and feel the high energy. The waning period is a time to go within and seek shamanic wisdom in quiet ways. The closer the waxing moon gets to full, the more the energy rises. As soon as the full moon has passed, the energy also begins to wane. Therefore, it is best to raise energy during the waxing moon and let go of things during the waning moon. For instance, pray for increase of anything during the waxing moon and pray for letting go of something during the waning moon.

Likewise, we can also go about our everyday lives in synchronization with Moon's phases. This is not to say that you can't let go of things when the moon is waxing or that you cannot begin new projects when the moon is full. Sometimes life gives us no choice to time these things ex- actly. But if you can time things to coincide with Moon's various energies, the universe will be aligned in such a way as to facilitate all you do. You will become more "lucky," and life will seem to flow more smoothly and easily. Whenever you can, then, attune your life to Moon's phases.

Here I present a list of Moon's phases with their associated energies. (Moon charts and calendars that give the exact date of each moon phase for the year are available at most metaphysical bookstores. Many daily newspapers list the date of the full and new moon on the weather page.)

Sun Father, Moon Mother

Waxing Moon: From New To Full

New Moon—Plant positive ideas in your subconscious mind. Begin new projects. Renew hope and maintain a youthful outlook. Start new relationships. Pray and work for freedom and independence.

Waxing Crescent—Integrate New Moon energy into your life. Give full attention to new projects and dreams that were begun on the new moon. Nurture them and make them grow.

First Quarter—Attune to your own needs. The focus now is self-renewal as we build self-love and self-confidence.

Waxing Gibbous—Focus on individual expression. Let creativity flow and flourish. Undertake or continue artistic pursuits.

Full Moon—This is the time of fulfillment of wishes, dreams and desires. This is also a good time to attract love, friendship and abundance, a time to give thanks and celebrate life.

Waning Moon: From Full to New

Waning Gibbous—Inspire and help others. Use this time to give, to help and to attune yourself to the needs of others.

Last Quarter—This is a time of healing dreams and deep meditation. Look within to tap inner power.

Waning Crescent—Practice trancing, divination, seeing the future and remembering past lives. Psychic abilities flow; mysterious and hidden secrets become known.

CHAPTER 10

THE DREAMTIME

SPIRIT DREAMS

Long before the advent of psychotherapy, tribal peoples not only took dreams seriously, they held them in high regard. Some native peoples even considered the dreamtime to be every bit as valid and "real" as the state of waking awareness. So they didn't just analyze dreams; they regarded them as profoundly important communications with and from the spirit world. Since dreams are a major way that the Spirit Beings, Nature Spirits and the Creator speak to us, primal people with a special gift for dreaming were and are considered to be very important to the welfare of the tribe.

Primal peoples also believe that dreams provide the answers to our problems and solutions to what goes wrong in our lives, for the Spirit Beings and the collective unconscious have all the wisdom of the universe at their command.

155

Shamanic Wisdom

We on a shamanic path are continually seeking guidance from Spirit, from that which is wise and sacred. Our dreams are a major avenue of this guidance. In the mainstream Western culture, where dreams are less highly regarded, we have to make a special effort to integrate these powerful spirit messages into our lives. No one on a shamanic path can ignore or dismiss them ("Well, it was only a dream!"). We can learn from tribal peoples to receive the gift of dreams and incorporate this gift into our own spiritual growth.

Many people find it helpful to share their dreams with family members or friends as soon as they wake. Such sharing establishes the importance of our dreams for ourselves and the circle of people with whom we most closely share our lives. And their insights into our dreams, over a period of time, will help us understand what a particular dream might be telling us or asking of us. In these dream sharing sessions, the emphasis falls less on the "correct" interpretation and more on how a dream affects our lives and the lives of those around us. (Persons working alone will find that keeping a written journal of dreams will substitute, to some extent, for the group of "dreamkeepers" just described.)

Shamanic wisdom holds that messages to us from the spirit world ask for a "making real." That means we should try to see what it is they are asking us to do and then put that into effect. This may be done literally or symbolically, either ritualizing our dreams by acting them out in a ceremony or making them real in a mundane, practical sense.

For example, Black Elk, the famous Oglala holy

man, became very ill as a child. During his illness he had a great vision, but he did not share or act on this vision in any way. Many years later, when he was a young man, he had a psychological crisis. When the traditional healer who was treating him unearthed the story of his great vision, it became apparent that Black Elk must "make real" the message from the spirit world in order to bring harmony into his own life. So a spectacular ceremony was performed, with all the members of the band taking a part in acting out the vision. Then Black Elk found that he had great spirit powers at his disposal. Dreams also call out for this type of "making real." The spirit messages given us through dreams and visions are given to beings on the earth plane so that we can make the message manifest here. This brings harmony to the spirit world and to the earth as well.

Besides holding ceremonies that re-enact the people's dreams to bring spirit and earth into harmony, native wisdom also holds that dreams manifest an inner desire of the soul. Therefore, some primal groups hold dream ceremonies where people tell of a dream that has great meaning to them. Everyone else offers feedback and interpretation. Then the entire tribe helps the dreamer realize the soul wish in the dream. If the wish cannot be realized on a practical level (like violence, for example), then it is acted out— with the people playing different parts of the dream. Thus, one way or another, the dream is made real.

This is very much like modern psychological dreamwork. But shamanic wisdom teaches us that people can get together without a formal therapist and explore the dreamtime with each other

When we do dreamwork with our family and friends,

157

with our "dreamkeepers," we should first thank the spirit world for the gift of the dream. Then we should tell it or act it out with the group. Sometimes we are not able immediately to interpret the meaning of our dreams. Yet, if we ritualize the dream anyway, the meaning will often clarify itself by the very process of enacting it. This occurs because the significance of a dream often becomes more quickly apparent when we and other people take on the roles of the characters in the dream and speak from those perspectives. (Again, the same approach can be used in a dream journal by writing freely from the viewpoint of a given dream character.)

Dream Enactment

Each group participant takes on the role of a being or object in the dreamer's dream. (Objects can speak and interact in the enactment.) The dreamer is the main protagonist and director. Then everyone "play-acts" their roles, allowing the dreamer to lead the way, to be the star, to change direction and even to change which character he or she portrays in mid-enactment.

Each group member has a dream or an important part of a dream enacted. At first this might seem awkward or hilarious, but with practice, great insights into dreams can occur.

Some dreams are sufficiently important to be acted out ritually, too. This often suggests itself naturally as an extension of discussions with our dreamkeeping group or our insights while writing in our dream journal.

If a dream is very important to you and also has

158

The Dreamtime

archetypal messages that are universal, then a dreamgroup might decide to create a ceremony around the dream. For instance, I dreamed that Earth Mother, personified as a woman in a flowing green robe, came to me and told me to build a women's peace lodge. This lodge would bring the harmony of the spirit world to earth. In the dream I did this with a group of women, at night, during a full moon. We built a circular lodge in the rainforest out of palm fronds. Then soldiers lined up and asked entrance to the lodge. We women took away their weapons and uniforms. When each soldier stood naked before the lodge entrance and vowed to be peacemakers henceforth, we women dressed the men as Earth Mother, in flowing robes. Then we allowed them entrance to the lodge.

My dreamgroup decided to ritualize this dream. The gazebo in my yard became the peace lodge. On a full moon night the women of the group brought offerings that represented peace and decorated the lodge with them. Then the men of the group lined up and asked for entrance. Instead of laying down weapons, they each pledged to work in some way for inner or outer peace. Then they disrobed and the women dressed them in flowing robes and decorated them with symbols of peace. Only then were they allowed to enter the peace lodge, where we had a gentle discussion of all the ways we can all strive for peace. Each participant was moved and transformed in deep ways during this ritual.

When you ritualize a dream, you are trying to instil the spirit message into the heart of all the participants. Each participant then receives an important insight or message from Spirit.

Shamanic Wisdom

If we are to be empowered as fully as possible by our dreams, we have to become more conscious in our dream activity. Shamanic wisdom stresses the importance of lucid dreaming. Some of us have kept this ability alive from our childhoods, the ability to interact with our dreams while we are dreaming. But all of us can learn or relearn this most powerful of ways to receive dreamed guidance.

Lucid Dreaming.

As you are lying down to sleep, as you are entering the twilight world between dreams and waking, tell yourself that you will expect and welcome your dreams. Tell the spirits that you are ready to communicate with them while you are dreaming. Affirm, to yourself, that you can participate in your dreams....Then, when you awaken slightly during the night in the middle of a dream, begin imagining, visualizing or fantasizing how that dream should continue or change in a way that is more rewarding or exciting. Do this each time you awaken from a dream, or anytime you are dreaming and suddenly realize you are doing so. When you wake up in the morning, thank the dream spirits for letting you enter their world in a conscious way.

Eventually the controlled lucidity will carry over into sleep. Ultimately you will be able to direct your dreams without waking up first.

Lucid dreaming can be done by those who want to change nightmares into good experiences and by those who want to make good dreams even more wonderful, adventurous or magical. Lucid dreaming is also a good way to get past the cultural conditioning that causes us to consider nightmares as "bad dreams." Lucid dreamers know that a falling dream isn't an invitation to panic, for example. It's an invitation to keep falling, to fly to entirely new places and insights. And when a lucid dreamer encounters fearful beings, he or she knows how to approach them, how to remain open to the messages they have to bring. Therefore, it is best not to change every fearful dream into a safe and happy one. The spirits often use dreams to show us our own fears and other aspects of our shadow side. When we face these fearful situations or beings in a dream, we can then come to terms with, integrate and heal our own inner demons. So a lucid dreamer interacts with those images, too, learning from them and thanking the spirits for them. When we are able to dream lucidly, we can choose whether to face those inner shadows or to change the dream. If you can face them, you will be empowered in the process. Or you can choose to have fantastic dreams experiences that are rich and very satisfying. In lucid dreaming, so-called bad dreams begin to reveal themselves as integral to our understanding, and so-called good dreams become pathways to ecstasy.

Lucid dreaming transforms dreaming into a most potent tool for our own spiritual growth and transformation. It brings sacred power and deep insight into our dreaming lives and into our lives in the waking world as well.

RAINBOW MEDICINE

The magical effects of various colors figures in the practices of those who walk a shamanic path. Many native people will identify with a color, for it will not only represents something they stand for, it will also invoke that color's medicine power in its bearer. Indeed, some people seem to resonate with a particular color or color combination. In your own exploration of rainbow medicine you should become aware, first of all, of what each color means for you—how you resonate (or not) with that color. And this will vary from individual to individual. For example, black suggests the mystery and wonder of the night for some; for others, it is a color associated with depression or even evil.

Most of us tend subconsciously to select a color that reflects and expresses our basic orientation to life. For instance, a person who is often depressed may wear somber colors, thus reinforcing a tendency towards pessimism or depression. To alter our energy field in more positive directions, then, we should select for ourselves a color that reinforces a more positive stance.

That's why I wear green. It represents my own connection to nature and especially to my relatives among the growing green beings of the earth. To me, it is the color or Earth Mother and it says that I stand for Her and stand up for Her. And its particular rainbow medicine, or energy frequency, helps me sustain the energy I need to do that.

My friend Coyote wears blue. This color, to him, stands for freedom. Love and defense of freedom are his spiritual alignments. He makes a stand for freedom at all times and wears blue to attract an energy to him that is wide and free as the sky.

You can also choose a color that represents what you stand for, and wear it often. And in addition to your basic or primary color medicine you may also use other colors for particular purposes. For instance, although my clothes and decor tend to be green, my bedroom is completely white. That's because, for me, white represents spiritual seeking, and I use this room whenever I meditate or go on spirit journeys indoors.

The powers we associate with colors can also be called upon to meet the needs of a particular moment, to invoke a particular sort of energy. To do this, you need only to visualize yourself and your aura awash in whatever color feels most appropriate in a given situation.

Finally, we can also surround ourselves with colors that will attract their associated medicine properties to us. For instance, if you associate reds and pinks with love and romance, then wearing these colors will help you attract those things.

Below are some correspondences between colors and the properties which are commonly associated with them. It is a place to start, but you should work out your own list of colors and their medicine powers, basing it on your own discoveries.

Blue: Serenity, peace, calmness, intuition.
Light Blue: Meditation, psychic ability, compassion.
Brown: Strength, stability, practicality, acquiring land.
Green: Money, prosperity, abundance,
career success.

Light Green: Health, new beginnings, looking and feeling younger.
Orange: Energy, optimism, positive thoughts, cheerfulness.
Pink: Friendship, caring, affection, devotion, tenderness.
Purple: Success, confidence, spiritual attainment.
Red: Love, romance, passion, courage, enthusiasm, excitement.
White: Purity, truth, hope, harmony, spiritual enlightenment.
Yellow: Happiness, luck, intelligence, academic achievement.

WORDS OF POWER

One of the more accessible ways people in our mainstream culture can begin the process of developing medicine power is learning to use words as the vehicles of that power. We may already know how to do this, and we may call it verbal affirmations. In any case, traditional teachings stress the fact that words are rooted in breath and that breath is life. The spoken word, therefore, can carry with it the power of life itself.

Words spoken out loud and repeated with conviction have great medicine power. When we combine these words of power with visualizations, emotions and will, we then have very powerful medicine indeed. But the words alone can also be effective. For example, one of my students could not visualize or even feel very much. His imagination and heart were blocked. But he could speak. So this is where he was able to begin—with words of power. He was in his early twenties and had never had a girlfriend. He wanted one very much. He began to create that reality verbally through words of power. He began to state, out loud, in a confident, powerful voice, affirmations like, "I am attractive to women. I have a lot of love to give. I am now ready to have an intimate relationship." He wrote out his own affirmations and repeated them many times a day. He was very serious about it. Only a few weeks later he met a woman and began a romantic relationship with her.

Words of power can be used to affirm and create anything you wish to change for the better in your life: to attract love and friends; to overcome bad habits; to open yourself to abundance, success, health and happiness. The key to all this is stating these affirmations confidently, frequently and positively. Also, it is important to state them as if the reality you affirm is already present. So you might say, "I have abundance in my life now" rather than "I am not poor anymore." To be sure, our subconscious selves and the natural powers respond to positives rather than negatives. And the "now" emphasizes the need for the reality to begin manifesting itself at once, not sometime in the indefinite future.

It helps, too, if you not only speak these affirmations aloud and often but if you visualize them as well. For example, while affirming abundance, visualize abundance in your life. Or while affirming confidence, "see" yourself behaving confidently.

Keep repeating your words of power in various ways all day long, for we are trying to change attitudes and habits that had many years to root themselves. Sing them in the shower, shout them in the car, whisper them as you fall off to sleep, awaken with them as your first words of the day. We should continue repeating our words of power and visualizations even after the new reality begins to make itself evident in our lives.

When you repeat your words of power often, you may well find that they are shaping themselves into a chant or song accompanied, perhaps, by a melody or syncopated beat. This is very powerful medicine and will help the words of power take effect since our subconsious selves and the Nature Spirits are very much attuned to rhythmic expressions of all kinds. The melody may change after a while. If it does, let it. In fact, you may find the words of affirmation also changing with time and repitition. Songs such as these are given to us by the spirits and are very sacred. Unlike the songs you hear on the radio, your song will probably have only one or two lines and a very simple melody. It may or may not rhyme. If you are given a song, or if your words of power become a song, sing your sacred song often.

You can also experiment with joining your affirmative words of power to one or more natural powers. For example, you might find it helpful to stand outdoors on a windy day and chant your affirmations. In doing so, the forcefulness of expression you affirm will join with the forces of the Wind Spirits. All your words of power might be appropriately strengthened by joining them with the energies of Sun, Moon, rain, flowing water, flowering plants and so forth.

The Dreamtime

Sending Words Of Power With Smoke Spirits

Light some sage, pine or other incence. Pray to the spirit of the herb you burn to send your prayer to the Great Spirit. Now send a voice of power into the smoke. Watch your strong voice move the smoke. See your words of power go into the smoke and then rise up and go forth to the universe.

Sending Words Of Power With Water Spirits

When bathing, showering, swimming or standing in the rain, ask the Water Spirits to send your voice of power to Earth Mother. Then affirm with confidence and with visualizations, sending your voice into the water. This presents opportunites of chanting, singing and affirming your words of power whenever you bathe.

The last, and perhaps the most important, thing to learn in using words of power is to speak only truthful words at all times. To use words of power effectively and to walk a shamanic path in general, your word is your will. Because the shamanic path connects you to your own deepest self, to the collective subconscious of all living beings, to the Nature Spirits and to Earth Mother, what you say at all times is taken seriously by these spirits and forces. If your words are untrue, they will not take you seriously, you will not take yourself seriously and you will have trouble manifesting reality with your spoken voice. Chanting, words of power, sacred singing and even praying with words will not be very effective. In this path, your word is truly your bond.

Shamanic Wisdom

So learn to use words wisely and with great regard for yourself and others. The most powerful words, after all, are the most gentle ones. Life is nurtured in gentleness, not in anger. Therefore speak so that you heal in gentle and life-affirming ways.

CHAPTER 11
LIGHT AND SHADOW

BECOMING YOUR OWN SHAMAN

Does embracing a shamanic worldview mean that you can or must become a shaman? That you hang out a shingle that identifies you as such to the rest of society? That you set up an office, hire a receptionist and accept Visa and Mastercard for shamanic services rendered?

I don't think so. Traditional shamans are produced by societies in which shamanism plays a distinct and well-defined role in the overall scheme of things. The culture produces the shaman, regulates the shaman's activities and legitimates the shaman's claims. Modern industrial cultures are geared to produce many things and offer many roles. But shamans are not one of them. Or, to put it bluntly, there's an awful lot of room here (and absolutely no checks and balances against) charlatans, con men and liars.

Nevertheless, all of us born of Earth Mother have been given shamanic gifts. By practicing Nature Spiritual-

Shamanic Wisdom

ity and learning from those who do, you can develop those gifts to the fullest. Shamanic empowerment is open to everyone, for it is a gift given to us by our sacred Earth Mother. And because there are no valid shamans in our culture, each and every one of us must become our own shaman. You can balance and bring wholeness to yourself and your pets and, yes, the earth, too. You can journey to the spirit realm and return with a true vision. You can communicate directly with all beings of nature, and you can learn to see in a sacred manner (our culture calls this psychic ability). You can learn to look within for wisdom and guidance, to become a peacemaker and earth-healer, to practice shamanism in the environment where you are and to become fully empowered and whole.

This is no small accomplishment. Consider for a moment the scale of destruction that has been wrought in the name of progress. Make a list of the toxins in the air you breathe and the water you drink. List the toxic waste dumps in your own locale. List the animals and birds which have come to face extinction in your lifetime. List the native peoples who have been decimated or rubbed out entirely in the name of progress—in the last two hundred years and even today. Now ask yourself if becoming a shaman and healer for Earth Mother, even on a modest scale and in a quiet way, is important.

When you become your own shaman, then you are beginning a life of individual empowerment, inner-directed seeking and alliance with the life force itself. You are entering a life which does not necessarily require you to dress in exotic costumes and practice exotic rituals, but does require you to put on new perceptions and work

170

Light and Shadow

actively for the benefit of all living beings.

In this culture, that is a revolutionary act. Not only are you rejecting the world-destroying greed which calls itself progress, you are rejecting imposed authority of all kinds. Rather than seeking out the Expert or Guru or Shaman who will tell you what to do and how to live, you are seeking to learn those things from Earth Mother herself, from the wisdom of all the species and from your own deep, inner wisdom. When each of us knows that we can journey to the spirit world, learn the truth there and return with the courage to act on that truth, the need for outer authorities and experts disappears and the real healing of the Earth—and ourselves—begins.

Yet even as this process begins, we must be clear about who we are, what we are doing and why we are doing it. To become our own shaman for ourselves and Earth Mother is not the same as practicing shamanism in a traditional culture. Perhaps this brief story will illustrate the difference.

Many years ago, before I or most of us in our culture even knew the word "shamanism," I saw a television program about native people in South America. Tribal life was in transition; the tribe could not make a living off the land anymore because all the trees had been cut down and the land was despoiled. The tribal people made a meager living doing manual labor for the mainstream society. They worked long, hard hours each day. The thing that impressed me, bowled me over, was the tribe's shaman. He too trudged home exhausted after the workday, for he had to work also. He wore workman's clothing, with no tribal decorations at all. But when he got back, he began healing the people—for free. After he'd seen the patients who needed him for that evening, he then gathered together little sapling trees and the implements with which to plant them. He'd grown these little trees himself, at his own expense and effort. Then all alone, a bundle of trees and planting tools strapped to his back, bent and old and tired, he trudged into the jungle as it began to grow dark to replant the trees. I have never forgotten having seen a real shaman. I always keep him in mind when I meet a self-proclaimed, non-indigenous "shaman" wearing expensive, custom-made, fake Indian outfits and jewelry and talking New Age babble. I always keep him in mind if I'm ever tempted to think of myself as a shaman.

To follow a shamanic path and to become one's own and Earth Mother's shaman is a noble path that we can all walk, but to call oneself a shaman for the people means meeting an exceedingly high standard. I have personally never met anyone who met the standard of that shaman. I live in the East Bay of San Francisco where nearly every other person I meet is a self-proclaimed, money-charging shaman. However, I suspect that I have never met a genuine shaman.

THE BALANCE

To be in balance and harmony means accepting, totally and ecstatically, all that is—the struggle as well as the vision, the pain as well as the joy. On a shamanic path we embrace the mysterious wonder of this great gift of life Earth Mother has given us; we learn to transcend, too, the physical limitation of our bodies and the drama that is living. This path teaches us to face the whole of reality, light and shadow, with dignity and courage.

Some teachers and writers these days seem to suggest that we can be happy all the time—if only we will get this or that therapy, embrace this or that philosophy, practice this or that spiritual path. They promise a kind of Never-Never Land. They're wrong. Or they're stretching the truth while not-so-incidentally fattening both their egos and their checking accounts. A life of fulfillment is a life filled with the full range of human emotions and experiences—lived in balance and harmony.

It is never easy for any of us to deal with the shadowy aspects of our existence. We ask why living beings must suffer, why we live by taking the lives of other living beings for our food, our clothes, our shelter. And even if we achieve a state of total balance with the natural world, we would still experience some emotional or physical pain from time to time; we would still be fed and nurtured by the sacrifices of other creatures. On a shamanic path we recognize the truth that we are always involved with a mixture of light and darkness. We accept that because we accept the gift of life itself.

The rain forests which are filled with shadows and dangerous animals and poisonous snakes are, for peoples like the pygmies, a place which defines and nurtures their lives. The same jungle which could kill them feeds them and provides all their other needs. To us, they seem to dwell in small clearings of light surrounded by a perilous darkness. To them, becuase they know how to live harmoniously there, they are simply at home.

Even the most enlightened individuals, the strong-

Shamanic Wisdom

est families and the most efficient societies live surrounded by some darkness too. That is the reality of human life on this planet. If we embrace the darkness as part of the Great Gift and integrate it into our lives (as the pygmies seem to do), we not only strike a balance; we attain true power. When we deny the darkness, push it away or repress it, we get into trouble. At the individual level, such denial produces addiction, mental illness or worse. At the social level, such repression produces genocide, the destruction of the natural environment and the ever-present possibility of nuclear annihilation.

Modern religions seem to pit humans against nature and humans against our own nature. These same religions project the shadow within each of us to create the evil "out there": the Enemy, the Sinful, Satan. Earth Religions, because they embrace the shadow within, have no need for a Satan "out there." In such religions, natural impulses are accepted for what they are, not rejected as evil promptings from the devil. In this way, all the forces of the physical universe and the psychic universe alike are seen as part of a seamless whole. Therefore, no single force or impulse becomes distorted and dangerous because it has been filled with the projected energies of denial.

In repressions, projection and denial life is destroyed. In acceptance, and in harmony, and in balance, life goes on.

CHAPTER 12
ECO-MAGIC

Those of us who walk a shamanic path realize that we are all related and that relatives look out for each other. We appeal to the nature forces for wisdom, power, health and happiness. And in return we steward and protect all of nature--Wind, Animal, Air, Bird, Tree, Water--all Earth Mother's creation.

Here is a brief list to get you started in the caretaking of Earth Mother. This is the greatest shamanic wisdom of all, for as you save the earth, you save yourself. Remember, all healing begins with healing Her. All power begins with reempowering our sacred Earth Mother. For the Earth is your mother, and you are the Earth.

May you heal and balance and protect and give joy to Earth Mother as you heal and balance and protect and give joy to yourself!

Cut all six plastic six-pack holder rings with a scissors

before you throw them away. Birds and sea creatures can get their necks stuck in the plastic rings that hold beer, soda and similar packaging.

Avoid the use of styrofoam. It will still be here hundreds of years from now. It does not break down and biodegrade.

Never buy ivory. Elephants are being slaughtered for ivory, and are on the verge of extinction.

Do not buy products made from endangered species, such as coral, tortoise shell, snake skin and so forth.

Do not buy fur coats.

Carpool, take public transportation, walk, or ride a bike whenever possible.

Do not support any business which imprisons a dolphin or a whale (seaquariums, swimming with dolphins). These sacred beings are at least as intelligent as you and I, and should be at least as free.

Do not support the circus. Animals are not put here by the Great Spirit to perform at the crack of a whip.

Wash dishes in a pan or sink full of water. Washing them in running water is very wasteful of water.

Eco-Magic

Keep your car well tuned. In doing so, you help lessen the amount of carbon dioxide emitted into the atmosphere. Carbon dioxide is creating the greenhouse effect.

Use phosphate-free detergents. Phosphates are killing our lakes and streams.

Set your lawn mower on high. A close cropped lawn requires more watering. Leave grass clippings and shredded leaves on lawn after mowing. They will hold in moisture and disintegrate into fertilizer.

Recycle glass, bottles, cans, paper and plastic.

Use organic pesticides on garden and lawn.

Plant a tree. Call your local county extension agent to find out the best trees to plant in your area.

Tune your furnace. This can cut down on chemical emissions that cause acid rain and the greenhouse effect.

Grow house plants in your home and office. The spider plant absorbs formaldehyde fumes.

Releasing helium balloons is not festive or fun for the sea creatures who eat them and die. Whenever you hear about a balloon release in your area, contact the folks involved and explain this to them.

Don't use aluminum foil. If you do use it, wash and

Shamanic Wisdom

reuse it.

Plant berry bushes and fruit trees for yourself and the wildlife in your area.

Buy non-halon fire extinguishers. Halons destroy the ozone layer whether or not the fire extinguisher is ever used, because halons leak from the extinguisher.

Store your refrigerated food in reusable containers. This will cut down on your use of plastic bags, plastic wrap and aluminum foil.

Just say no to car air conditioners. Air conditioned cars leak CFCs, thereby depleting the ozone layer. They also exacerbate the greenhouse effect and require a car to guzzle more gas.

Turn water off while shaving.

Use cloth napkins. Paper napkins kill trees!

Use unbleached coffee filters, found in health food stores. The process of bleaching them (and paper towels and other paper products) releases dioxin into the environment. Use washable cloths to wipe up spills in the kitchen instead of paper towels.

Buy latex paint for your house. Oil based paints create very toxic pollutants when they are manufactured.

Eco-Magic

Bring a reusable cloth bag to the grocery store with you. This saves on paper and plastic tote sacks.

When out hiking or camping, stay on the paths. Don't hike through the brush, destroying the flora and fauna as you go.

Buy organic produce. Your local health food store will carry organic products. By supporting organic farmers, you help put an end to farming with pesticides.

Start your own organic garden. This is a wonderful way to be in nature. Home grown produce tastes delicious!

When hiking or camping, do not pick or take anything with you. Leave it just the way it is. Do not topple dead trees for firewood. These are the homes of many birds and small animals.

Use rechargeable batteries, or better yet , recycle your batteries. Small household batteries, the kind used in portable radios, flashlights, etc., can become very toxic heavy metal poisoners once they end up at the dump or landfill.

Compost your food scraps and leftovers.

Save water while brushing teeth by turning off the tap until you rinse your mouth.

Shamanic Wisdom

Avoid mothballs. They emit harmful chemicals into the atmosphere.

Be fire safe at all times. We have lost much wildland and wildlife due to carelessness.

Shop locally, whenever possible. Support your small neighborhood stores. It costs more economically and environmentally to drive to the mall than it does to walk or bike to the little neighborhood store.

Pick up litter in natural places.

Help a stray cat or dog. If you cannot keep it yourself, bring it to a vet, get it shots and place an ad in the paper. Interview prospective owners carefully. I have done this many times, and it has been very emotionally rewarding to see a pitiful stray blossom under my care and then find a good home. If you are considering taking the stray to an animal shelter, find out if that shelter kills the unadopted ones. Many do. Humans domesticated the dog and the cat, and it is therefore our responsibility to care for them. It is our sacred duty to help all domesticated animals who have been abandoned. And it is a fallacy that cats can survive on their own; they cannot.

Don't use commercial pet flea collars. These collars create toxins during the manufacturing process and chemical pollution when they are thrown away. Health food stores often carry alternative, safe flea remedies. Many people feed their pets garlic or brewer's yeast, and find that this helps to repel fleas.

Vote green. Educate yourself on evironmental issues and vote for politicians who support the environment. Don't be fooled by empty rhetoric. It is "in" to give lip service. Look at their record. Vote politicians out if they don't measure up.

Help save the rainforests. More than fifty percent of Earth Mother's wildlife live in tropical rainforests, which are fast being wiped out. The rainforests produce a large percentage of the earth's oxygen and provide us with many life saving drugs and health treatments. To find out how you can help write: The Rainforest Action Network, 301 Broadway, Suite A, San Francisco, California, 94133. (415)398-4404.

Buy cruelty-free cosmetics and personal grooming items. Many cosmetic companies conduct extremely cruel, painful and useless animal experiments. However, there are companies that do not experiment on animals at all. Your local health food store probably carries some of these items. Or you can write for a list of cruelty free companies to: People For The Ethical Treatment Of Animals, P.O. Box 42516, Washington D.C., 20015

Stop unnecessary animal experimentation. Much of the cruel and torturous laboratory animal experimentation is needless. The experiments are often simply a feeble excuse to obtain grant money. The experiments are often useless, stupid, repeat experiments and unbelievably cruel.

For further infortmation write to: People For The Ethical Treatment of Animals at the above address.

Educate yourself about various environmental interest groups. For example, Greenpeace is devoted to stopping the exploitation and degradation of the environment through nonviolent means. Greenpeace was active in stopping the worldwide commercial and scientific slaughter of whales and responsible for halting the clubbing of baby harp seals. Greenpeace is funded entirely by individual contributions; and does not accept government or corporate donations because they feel that it might compromise their decision making. If you wish to find out more about this organzation write: Greenpeace U.S.A., 1436 U Street, N.W., Washington D.C., 20009

ABOUT THE AUTHOR

Dolfyn cares deeply about nature. Her concern expresses itself in her writing and in her active involvement with environmental and earth stewardship issues. Her writings grow naturally from her practical experience in teaching, exploring and advocating for nature and the Nature Spirits.

Workshops With Dolfyn

Dolfyn teaches workshops and classes on Nature Spirituality and Shamanism in the San Francisco Bay area and nationally. For information, write: Earthspirit, Inc., 6114 La Salle Ave., Suite 362, Oakland, CA 94611

BOOKS BY DOLFYN:

CRYSTAL WISDOM: SPIRITUAL PROPERTIES OF CRYSTALS AND GEMSTONES - Beautifully written, this is a clear, comprehensive yet easy-to-read guide toward greater insight and deeper understanding of the spiritual values and potentials of crystals and gemstones. **CRYSTAL WISDOM** stresses your natural ability to communicate directly with crystals and other spirit stones without the need to master complex systems. This joyous book is a loving and friendly guide to tapping your own crystal wisdom.

Earthspirit Inc. offers the above book for $9.95 plus $2 shipping and handling. Send $11.95 in check or money order to: Earthspirit Inc., 6114 La Salle Ave., Suite 362, Oakland, CA 94611

AUDIO CASSETTES BY DOLFYN:

SHAMANISM: A GUIDE TO DEVELOPING SACRED POWER
This cassette covers aspects of shamanism common to native and tribal people the world over, yet applicable to our own lives. How to: create a Medicine Wheel, go on a Vision Quest, retrieve your Animal Spirit Guardians, develop sacred power and more.

CRYSTAL WISDOM: A BEGINNER'S GUIDE - This cassette inspires the beginner with all he or she needs to know to get started with crystals. Dolfyn teaches the basic aspects of crystal lore, such as tuning, healing, protecting, meditating, invoking with crystals.

Earthspirit, Inc. offers the above cassettes for $9.95 each. Send check or money order to 6114 La Salle Ave., Suite 362, Oakland, CA 94611

BOOKLETS BY DOLFYN:

BOUGH DOWN: PRAYING WITH TREE SPIRITS - Protective, wise, loving and strong, the Tree Spirits stand ready to help us, heal us, protect us. "Bough Down" teaches how to communicate directly with trees in order to benefit from their healing guidance and love.

PRAYING WITH FIRE: COMMUNICATING WITH FIRE SPIRITS - Fire Spirits respond to us, for in the human heart our own warmth and passion is akin to theirs. "Praying With Fire" teaches how to communicate with Fire and pray with this beautiful element.

CRYSTAL CONNECTION: FINDING YOUR SOULMATE - This remarkable book was channeled through a quartz crystal. The beings who wrote "Crystal Connection" describe themselves as a crystal, a space being and a goddess. With great love and wisdom they weave together a book of beauty, inspiration and practical application. "Crystal Connection" covers how to find one's soulmate.

SHAMANISM AND NATURE SPIRITUALITY: THE SACRED CIRCLE -Emphasizes self-created circle ceremonies of life affirmation, with the step by step guidance necessary to cast a sacred circle.

SHAMANISM: A BEGINNER'S GUIDE - With clarity and simplicity, Dolfyn discusses those basic aspects of shamanism which are common to native and tribal people the world over: Creating a medicine wheel or sacred circle, raising medicine power, going on a spirit journey, meeting your animal spirit guardians, and more.

Earthspirit, Inc. offers the above five booklets as a set, for $14.95. Send check or money order to: 6114 La Salle Ave., Suite 362, Oakland, CA 94611